*The Trees
of Ashe County,
North Carolina*

CONTRIBUTIONS TO SOUTHERN APPALACHIAN STUDIES

1. *Memoirs of Grassy Creek: Growing Up in the Mountains on the Virginia–North Carolina Line.* Zetta Barker Hamby. 1998

2. *The Pond Mountain Chronicle: Self-Portrait of a Southern Appalachian Community.* Edited by Leland R. Cooper and Mary Lee Cooper. 1998

3. *Traditional Musicians of the Central Blue Ridge: Old Time, Early Country, Folk and Bluegrass Label Recording Artists, with Discographies.* Marty McGee. 2000

4. *W.R. Trivett, Appalachian Pictureman: Photographs of a Bygone Time.* Ralph E. Lentz II. 2001

5. *The People of the New River: Oral Histories from the Ashe, Alleghany and Watauga Counties of North Carolina.* Edited by Leland R. Cooper and Mary Lee Cooper. 2001

6. *John Fox, Jr., Appalachian Author.* Bill York. 2003

7. *The Thistle and the Brier: Historical Links and Cultural Parallels Between Scotland and Appalachia.* Richard Blaustein. 2003

8. *Tales from Sacred Wind: Coming of Age in Appalachia. The Cratis Williams Chronicles.* Cratis D. Williams. Edited by David Cratis Williams and Patricia D. Beaver. 2003

9. *Willard Gayheart, Appalachian Artist.* Willard Gayheart and Donia S. Eley. 2003

10. *The Forest City Lynching of 1900: Populism, Racism, and White Supremacy in Rutherford County, North Carolina.* J. Timothy Cole. 2003

11. *The Brevard Rosenwald School: Black Education and Community Building in a Southern Appalachian Town, 1920–1966.* Betty J. Reed. 2004

12. *The Bristol Sessions: Writings About the Big Bang of Country Music.* Edited by Charles K. Wolfe and Ted Olson. 2005

13. *Community and Change in the North Carolina Mountains: Oral Histories and Profiles of People from Western Watauga County.* Compiled by Nannie Greene and Catherine Stokes Sheppard. 2006

14. *Ashe County: A History; A New Edition.* Arthur Lloyd Fletcher. 2009 [2006]

15. *The New River Controversy; A New Edition.* Thomas J. Schoenbaum. Epilogue by R. Seth Woodard. 2007

16. *The Blue Ridge Parkway by Foot: A Park Ranger's Memoir.* Tim Pegram. 2007

17. *James Still: Critical Essays on the Dean of Appalachian Literature.* Edited by Ted Olson and Kathy H. Olson. 2008

18. *Owsley County, Kentucky, and the Perpetuation of Poverty.* John R. Burch, Jr. 2008

19. *Asheville: A History.* Nan K. Chase. 2007

20. *Southern Appalachian Poetry: An Anthology of Works by 37 Poets.* Edited by Marita Garin. 2008

21. *Ball, Bat and Bitumen: A History of Coalfield Baseball in the Appalachian South.* L.M. Sutter. 2009

22. *The Frontier Nursing Service: America's First Rural Nurse-Midwife Service and School.* Marie Bartlett. 2009

23. *James Still in Interviews, Oral Histories and Memoirs.* Edited by Ted Olson. 2009

24. *The Millstone Quarries of Powell County, Kentucky.* Charles D. Hockensmith. 2009

25. *The Bibliography of Appalachia: More Than 4,700 Books, Articles, Monographsand Dissertations, Topically Arranged and Indexed.* Compiled by John R. Burch, Jr. 2009

26. *Appalachian Children's Literature: An Annotated Bibliography.* Compiled by Roberta Teague Herrin and Sheila Quinn Oliver. 2010

27. *Southern Appalachian Storytellers: Interviews with Sixteen Keepers of the Oral Tradition.* Edited by Saundra Gerrell Kelley. 2010

28. *Southern West Virginia and the Struggle for Modernity.* Christopher Dorsey. 2011

29. *George Scarbrough, Appalachian Poet: A Biographical and Literary Study with Unpublished Writings.* Randy Mackin. 2011

30. *The Water-Powered Mills of Floyd County, Virginia: Illustrated Histories, 1770–2010.* Franklin F. Webb and Ricky L. Cox. 2012

31. *School Segregation in Western North Carolina: A History, 1860s–1970s.* Betty Jamerson Reed. 2011

32. *The Ravenscroft School in Asheville: A History of the Institution and Its People and Buildings.* Dale Wayne Slusser. 2014

33. *The Ore Knob Mine Murders: The Crimes, the Investigation and the Trials.* Rose M. Haynes. 2013

34. *New Art of Willard Gayheart.* Willard Gayheart and Donia S. Eley. 2014

35. *Public Health in Appalachia: Essays from the Clinic and the Field.* Edited by Wendy Welch. 2014

36. *The Rhetoric of Appalachian Identity.* Todd Snyder. 2014

37. *African American and Cherokee Nurses in Appalachia: A History, 1900–1965.* Phoebe Ann Pollitt. 2016

38. *A Hospital for Ashe County: Four Generations of Appalachian Community Health Care.* Janet C. Pittard. 2016

39. *Dwight Diller: West Virginia Mountain Musician.* Lewis M. Stern. 2016

40. *The Brown Mountain Lights: History, Science and Human Nature Explain an Appalachian Mystery.* Wade Edward Speer. 2017

41. *Richard L. Davis and the Color Line in Ohio Coal: A Hocking Valley Mine Labor Organizer, 1862–1900.* Frans H. Doppen. 2016

42. *The Silent Appalachian: Wordless Mountaineers in Fiction, Film and Television.* Vicki Sigmon Collins. 2017

43. *The Trees of Ashe County, North Carolina.* Doug Munroe. 2017

The Trees of Ashe County, North Carolina

Doug Munroe

CONTRIBUTIONS TO SOUTHERN APPALACHIAN STUDIES, 43

McFarland & Company, Inc., Publishers
Jefferson, North Carolina

Acknowledgments

Special thanks to my loving wife, Nancy Roten, for her many critiques, photographs and patient support.

To Betty Rembert for her masterful photography, enthusiasm, generosity, encouragement, consultations and many hours of driving around looking for photogenic trees in just the right light at just the right angle.

To Kelly Clampitt for her expert photographic vision, administrative help with all the photographs, critiques, field work and willingness to put up with my many requests for her time.

To Kim Hadley for squeezing time from her busy schedule to contribute her amazing photographic skills to this book.

To Robbie Franklin for planting the seed of this tree book that took only 17 years to germinate.

To Lisa Camp for her enthusiasm and photography and for keeping order.

Thanks also to Ron Joyner, Marty McGee, Cheryl Roberts, Scot Pope, Rex Miller and the late George Rembert II through his loving wife Betty for his photography.

I owe you all a trout dinner.

LIBRARY OF CONGRESS CATALOGUING-IN-PUBLICATION DATA

Names: Munroe, Doug, 1950– author.
Title: The trees of Ashe County, North Carolina / Doug Munroe.
Description: Jefferson, North Carolina : McFarland & Company, Inc., 2017. | Series: Contributions to southern Appalachian studies ; 43 | Includes index.
Identifiers: LCCN 2017041789 | ISBN 9781476672526 (softcover : acid free paper) ∞
Subjects: LCSH: Trees—North Carolina—Ashe County—Identification. | Trees—North Carolina—Identification.
Classification: LCC QK122.9 .M86 2017 | DDC 582.1609756—dc23
LC record available at https://lccn.loc.gov/2017041789

BRITISH LIBRARY CATALOGUING DATA ARE AVAILABLE

ISBN (print) 978-1-4766-7252-6   ISBN (ebook) 978-1-4766-3151-6

© 2017 Doug Munroe. All rights reserved

No part of this book may be reproduced or transmitted in any form or by any means, electronic or mechanical, including photocopying or recording, or by any information storage and retrieval system, without permission in writing from the publisher.

Front cover photograph of an old sugar tree in October by Betty Rembert; compare page 207

Printed in the United States of America

This is the second printing with Library of Congress data, recto photograph credits repositioned, and several corrections.

Edited by Robert Franklin;
designed by Jessica Wilcox and Robert Franklin; typeset by Jessica Wilcox

McFarland & Company, Inc., Publishers
Box 611, Jefferson, North Carolina 28640
www.mcfarlandpub.com

Table of Contents

Acknowledgments vi

Introduction 1

History 9

Part I: Evergreens

Broadleaf Evergreens 13
American Holly 13 ♦ *Rosebay Rhododendron* 15

Conifers 17
Carolina Hemlock 17 ♦ *White Pine* 18 ♦
Virginia Pine 21 ♦ *Table Mountain Pine* 21

Part II: Native Trees

The American Chestnut 23

The Beech Family 28
Chinquapin 29 ♦ *White Oak* 29 ♦ *Northern Red Oak* 32 ♦
Chestnut Oak 32 ♦ *American Beech* 34

The Other Nut Trees 39
Buckeye 39 ♦ *Black Walnut* 41 ♦ *Butternut* 44 ♦
Pignut Hickory and Shagbark Hickory 45

The Maples 49
Red Maple 49 ♦ *Sugar Maple* 53 ♦ *Black Maple* 56 ♦
Striped Maple 56 ♦ *Mountain Maple* 59

Table of Contents

The Birches   60
Yellow Birch 60 ♦ Black Birch 61 ♦
Blue Beech 63 ♦ Hophornbeam 65

The Magnolias   67
Tulip Tree 67 ♦ Wahoo 69 ♦ Cucumber Tree 70

The River Trees   72
Black Willow 72 ♦ Balsam Poplar 73 ♦ Sycamore 75

The Cherries   79
Black Cherry 79 ♦ Pin Cherry 80 ♦ Choke Cherry 80

Serviceberry   82

Sassafras   85

Staghorn Sumac   89

Ash   92
American White Ash 92 ♦ Mountain Ash 93

Linden   95

Tupelo or "Black Gum"   98

Hawthorn   101

Sourwood   104

Black/Yellow Locust   107

Witch Hazel   110

Flowering Dogwood   113

Poem: Bringing the Train to Todd   117

PART III: INTRODUCED TREES

Introduction   119

Ornamental Trees   124

Ginkgo   127

Dawn Redwood   131

Bald Cypress   134

The Spruces   137
Red Spruce 137 ♦ *Colorado Blue Spruce* 137 ♦
Norway Spruce 139 ♦ *White Spruce* 141 ♦
Oriental Spruce 142

The Cedars   144
Red Cedar 144 ♦ *Deodara* 146 ♦ *Atlantic Cedar* 147

False Cypress   150
Hinoki Cypress 150 ♦ *Boulevard and Cripps Cypress* 152 ♦
Alaskan Cedar 153 ♦ *Leyland Cypress* 153

Arborvitae   157

The Firs   159
Concolor Fir 159 ♦ *Momi Fir* 159 ♦ *Fraser Fir* 161

Ornamental Flowering Trees   164
Flowering Cherry 164 ♦ *Purple Leaf Plum* 164 ♦
Bloodgood Japanese Maple 166 ♦ *Fringe Tree* 167 ♦
Redbud 168 ♦ *Kousa Dogwood* 169 ♦ *Rose of Sharon* 171

Escaped Trees   173
Chinese Ailanthus 173 ♦ *Mimosa* 173 ♦
Big Tooth Aspen 174 ♦ *Paulownia* 175

Cottonwood and Weeping Willow   177

Crimson King Norway Maple   180

Ornamental Birches 182
River Birch 182 ♦ *European Birch 182* ♦
Paper Birch 185 ♦ *Asian Birch 186*

Ornamental Pears 188
Bradford 188 ♦ *Aristocrat 188*

Chinese Chestnut 190

Catawba Tree 193

Silver Maple 195

Part IV: Tree Culture

Tree Nursery 199

Four Seasons 206

Protected Land 215

Maple Syrup 219

Apples 227

Force of Nature 231

Christmas Tree Farming 236

Landscaping 241

Index 245

Introduction

In Ashe County, North Carolina, there is one unmistakable truth. Trees are everywhere they aren't. Although thousands of acres of land have been cleared of trees for farming, roads, lawns, power lines, buildings, ponds, and parking lots, they are massed everywhere else. If a vacant lot, meadow, or pasture is left unattended or neglected, trees will reseed it in a season and return it to forest in less than twenty years. Trees are relentless in their claim to these mountains. They are like an army on the border, ready to take over at the slightest opening.

The natural Ashe County landscape is dominated by trees as far as the eye can see.

Introduction

Trees are the keepers of the land in Ashe County. They are silent sentinels, except when the wind blows, and then they can be heard, soft as a whisper or loud as a train roaring by. Trees can be huge and majestic or small and dainty. They can be gnarled and twisted or straight and true. Smelly as a skunk or fragrant as a rose. Their wood can be as varied in color as a rainbow. Heavy as steel or light as aluminum. Trees semaphore the changing seasons. They hold soil and moisture in place. They take carbon and pollutants from the atmosphere and release oxygen back into it. They scent the air with fresh sweet aromas. They fertilize the soil with their decaying detritus.

Trees permeate our local culture thoroughly, yet they are nearly anonymous in their ubiquity. Few take the time to know one from the other, but in spite of that, trees are Ashe County's greatest treasure. We log them for their lumber, and ship it all over the world. We grow them for Christmas trees, garlands, and wreaths. We build our houses, barns, sheds, fences, furniture, musical instruments, tool handles, bridges, and picture frames from them. We carve them into sculptures, bowls, and walking sticks. We heat our homes

Betty Rembert

The fall woods become a kaleidoscope of changing colors that draw thousands of visitors to Ashe County every year.

Introduction

and shops with them. We tap some to make syrup and candy. We climb them and build treehouses in them. Hang swings and bird feeders from them. Pick their fruit and gather their nuts. Admire their flowers, leaves, limbs, and trunks. Paint pictures of them. Hide behind them. Plant them in our yards for beauty, shade, food, windbreaks, and privacy.

We give trees nicknames that conjure up folklore, songs, and poems: Sarvis, Tupelo, Wahoo, Hornbeam, Sassafras, Goosefoot, Ironwood, Shadblow, Saskatoon, and Buckeye. Unfortunately, most folks don't know a Hornbeam from a pole bean. The trees of Ashe County are its most valuable, prolific, diverse, and utilitarian resource no matter what the visionaries say about tourism and highways.

Ashe County is located in the northwest corner of North Carolina. It borders Virginia to the north, Tennessee to the west, and in-state, Watauga, Wilkes, and Alleghany counties to the south and east. It is part of the South-

An old road through the woods still invites a stroll to nowhere in particular.

ern Appalachian mountain range and butts up against the Eastern Continental Divide of North America where the Blue Ridge Parkway skirts the eastern edge of the county. Ashe County has an area of 406 square miles, and an exaggerated legend has it that it would be the largest county in the state if it were flattened out. The county's highest peak approaches a mile above sea level and in its lowest valley flows one of the oldest rivers on earth. The headwaters of the north fork of the New River originate in Ashe County along its border with Tennessee. The headwaters of the south fork of the New do not originate in Ashe County (but in Watauga), and the river meanders significantly across the eastern part of the county, flowing north to its confluence with the north fork just before entering Virginia.

There's plenty of water in these mountains. The trees of Ashe County receive between forty and sixty inches of rainfall a year. Not enough to call it a rainforest, but plenty enough when combined with ancient, eroded, nutrient-rich soil and thousands of years of plant and animal decay to support an antediluvian mixed hardwood forest.

There have been two distinct types of forest in Ashe County since the last Ice Age. The first, now mostly extinct in southern latitudes, was the boreal forest. A boreal forest is mainly a coniferous forest made up of spruce, fir, and pine, which are very cold-hardy. They had been pushed this far south during the last Ice Age by the glaciation just to the north in the Ohio Valley and in southern New York and Pennsylvania. As the earth warmed and the glaciers began to retreat, the boreal forest migrated along with the melting ice back to northern latitudes in Canada, leaving behind only remnant, relic patches of spruce and fir at the highest elevations. There is no boreal forest left in Ashe County but just to the north, Virginia's two highest elevation peaks, Mount Rogers and Whitetop Mountain, are capped with red spruce and Fraser fir. With the continued global warming, these stands of spruce and fir are endangered and will likely die out if the warming continues.

The next forest to emerge in Ashe County was the deciduous mixed hardwood forest. The transition from boreal forest to mixed hardwoods occurred over thousands of years and is still going on as is evidenced on the summits of Mount Rogers and Whitetop Mountain.

Introduction 5

As static as the forest appears in day-to-day life, it is anything but. It is always growing and changing for one reason or another. Global warming is just one of many complex forces of nature at play. Humans, mammals, insects, birds, reptiles, amphibians, fish, fungi, bacteria, and all sorts of microbiology are constantly in a life and death dance with trees. Drought, wind, and floods can wreak havoc on trees. Their exposure, whether it be north, east, south, or west, their elevation, whether it be mountaintop, mountain slope, or valley floor, and the soil type and pH, all factor into their success or failure. Amazingly, there is a variety of tree for every ecological niche in Ashe County.

Examples of how things can change dramatically in the tree world is a long list. Take the American Chestnut for instance. Chestnut was the dominant tree in the Appalachian Mountains for thousands of years, but in less than forty years, they were wiped out by a fungal blight in the first half of the

A very old Eastern Hemlock under attack from the hemlock woolly adelgid is still hanging on in a cemetery off Buck Mountain Road.

Eastern Hemlocks succumb to an infestation of hemlock woolly adelgid after thousands of years as a dominant evergreen in the Ashe County landscape.

twentieth century. It was a major catastrophe on many levels and nearly forgotten, but more on that later.

The Flowering Dogwood, North Carolina's state flower, once as common as Christmas trees, was nearly wiped out in the hardwood understory by another fungal blight in less than ten years.

The Yellow Locust is famous for its fast-growing rot resistant wood, honey made from its flowers, and long-burning firewood. A legendary tree known to last four days longer than stone, is now reduced by a tiny insect, a leaf miner, to a gnarly, dodey shadow of its former self.

The Eastern Hemlock, a towering evergreen tree in the Ashe County landscape, has been destroyed in the wild by a sapsucking little pissant of a bug called the hemlock woolly adelgid. Fortunately, the Eastern Hemlock's first cousin, the Carolina Hemlock, seems to be holding its own against the incipient adelgid in their cold, windy, high elevation coppices.

Ironically, thanks to an archaic, esoteric, spiritual custom of bringing an evergreen tree indoors to celebrate the winter solstice, the Fraser Fir, once a native boreal tree, has been reintroduced to the county by the Christmas tree industry. Though they do not grow in the wild now, they are the number one cash crop on Ashe County farms. When talking about the forces of nature, don't exclude farmers.

There are many more examples of the ever-changing make-up of the Ashe County forest, some of which will be visited in the pages to come. What is even more remarkable than the terrible losses of variety in the forest, is the adaptability of the trees that survive. Hardly anyone notices when an afflicted species disappears from the landscape, because other trees fill the niche so quickly. The trees of Ashe County abhor a void.

History

The trees of Ashe County have been here a long time and have adapted to the forces of nature and the desires of human nature with astonishing resilience. They have had to play musical chairs with who gets to be here now over and over and over again with stoic resolve. They were here long before any humans wandered by. It is hard to imagine what it must have looked like when those first people arrived. Buffalo and elk were here, whose trails the first Native Americans probably followed in their hunt for food, clothing, and shelter. The forest would have been spectacular old growth trees with thick trunks and high canopy. The New River would have been teeming with fish, fowl, and game. In addition to buffalo and elk there were wolves, mountain lions, otters, and eagles. All gone now. A perfect paradise except for old man winter. The first Native Americans probably didn't hang around for winter, just like the Floridians don't now. But they came in the warmer months and set up camps in the bottom land along the river. The natives hunted the Ashe County wilderness for thousands of years. All the while the Earth continued to warm and the forest migration, imperceptible to its inhabitants, continued its transition from boreal to hardwood forest.

The first European settlers arrived in Ashe County in a warmer time but they had to have been very hearty folks nonetheless. Enduring winter in the late seventeenth and early eighteenth centuries must have been an ordeal only the toughest, most resourceful settlers could pull off. At least there was plenty of firewood. They had to make do with the raw materials at hand, trees and stone, to build shelter for themselves and their livestock. Some folks used huge, old hollow trees to get out of the weather while they cleared land and built more permanent structures.

Unlike their Native American predecessors, early European settlers began to cut down trees in earnest to clear land for farming and buildings.

The Natives did do some clearing, too, with fire, but for different reasons: they burned the understory of the forest to clear it out for camps and hunting. They didn't have the metal tools it took to cut down big trees. As the number of European settlers increased, so did the clearing of land. The proverbial handwriting was on the wall as the old growth timber was cut down.

With the advent of the steam engine and the Industrial Revolution in the nineteenth century, the old growth forest in Ashe County was doomed. The arrival of the Virginia-Carolina railway in 1914 began the clear-cutting of 99 percent of the old growth trees. The only old growth trees left uncut were the trees growing on the highest ridges, above 4500 feet. The only reason they were not cut was that the trees were stunted and twisted at that elevation and undesirable for lumber. By 1928, all of the valuable timber was gone and along with the timber, most of the wildlife, too. It would take seventy years for some of the forest and wildlife to recover.

A once old growth forest can return to its former status, but it takes hundreds of years of being left alone to develop.

A dead, twisted old gnarly oak that managed to die of old age instead of a chain saw.

Once again the trees of Ashe County had to adjust to major changes, but instead of facing climate change over a long period of time, they had to adjust to human destruction over a short period of time. And adjust they did. Their stumps sprouted new growth, and the trees that remained dropped their seeds and re-sowed the cut-over land. The devastation of the clear-cut looked insurmountable, but the trees were indomitable. Mixed hardwood old growth forest takes hundreds of years to form, so the forest we see in 2017 has not had enough time to recover.

Fortunately, the state of North Carolina, the Nature Conservancy, the Blue Ridge Conservancy, and the New River Conservancy have all recognized the importance of protecting wild land, as in tens of thousands of acres, from development and logging. Leaving large tracts of wild land not only protects plant and animal habitat, it also protects the flow of vital, clean water. The state and conservancy organizations have worked both independently and collaboratively with state and private money to purchase land and conservation easements to accomplish this goal. Their work is ongoing and important for the common good and the health of everyone. Long-term protection of wild land will also allow the old growth forest to return to its natural state in the generations to come.

Part I: Evergreens

BROADLEAF EVERGREENS

That the mixed hardwood forest replaced the boreal forest is not to say there are no evergreen trees mixed in with the hardwoods. Most folks probably don't know there is a distinction between the hardwoods and the evergreens, so let's clear that up. In Ashe County–speak, hardwoods are trees that lose their leaves in the fall, and evergreens do not lose their leaves or needles. But it doesn't mean that all trees that lose their leaves have hard wood. Some of them don't. For example, a sugar maple is sometimes referred to as a rock maple, because its wood is hard and heavy. Whereas a red maple, a close cousin of the sugar maple, is referred to as a soft maple, because its wood is soft and light. All of the evergreens in Ashe County that are cone-bearing, known as conifers, are considered soft wood but instead of being called soft woods, they are called evergreens. Another Ashe County–speak about evergreens is all trees that have needles instead of leaves are called pines, whether they are pines or not.

Seven varieties of native evergreen trees live in Ashe County. Five of them are conifers, which means they make cones and have needles instead of flowers and leaves. They are White Pine, Virginia Pine, Table Mountain Pine, Eastern Hemlock, and Carolina Hemlock. The other two, American Holly and Rosebay Rhododendron, are broad-leaf evergreens.

American Holly

American Holly is native to the eastern half of Ashe County but doesn't occur at all in the western half of the county unless it is planted. Oddly, the Mountain Holly, a deciduous cousin of the American Holly, occurs in the western half of the county but not in the eastern half unless planted.

Part I: Evergreens

BETTY REMBERT

A female American Holly is a beautiful tree to look upon but not to touch. The leaves have sharp thorns.

American Hollies are dioecious, meaning they are gender specific, male and female, and only the females have berries. A mature female in full berry is a strikingly beautiful tree. Their dark green, horned, thorny leaves are a complementary backdrop for their fire engine red berries. Their boughs are traditional decorative fare during the winter holiday season but care must be taken handling them. Their stiff, spiny leaves can draw blood at the slightest poke and should be handled with heavy-duty gloves.

The wood of American Holly is nearly white in color and is often used as inlay in furniture and musical instruments. They are typically an understory tree in the mixed hardwood forest and seldom grow into a tree large enough for saw timber. So instead of sawn boards the Holly wood is derived from chunks of the trunk or stump.

As a landscape ornamental, the female American Holly is considered a specimen or focal point of garden design. A common mistake is to give them too little space to grow, not realizing they can reach thirty to forty feet in height and fifteen to twenty feet in width when planted in fertile soil and full sun.

Rosebay Rhododendron

Some would dispute the Rosebay Rhododendron's status as a tree by calling it a shrub, but in this book, it's a tree. Any woody plant that can reach a height of twenty feet is a tree. The Rosebay tends to grow in thickets called hells (the local word), but if you ever stood next to a Rosebay Rhododendron that is twenty feet tall, it certainly looks like a tree, not a shrub.

Rosebays are beautiful flowering trees. They introduce summer in Ashe County by beginning their bloom around the summer solstice. They tend to grow in impenetrable hells in the understory of hardwoods and, when combined with a steep slope, they are really difficult to navigate. Their showy pale white flowers emerge in trusses on the tips of their stems and seem to glow in the deep shade of summer woods. If there is such a thing as wood nymphs, as some folks believe, they surely live in a Rosebay hell.

Elegant Rosebay Rhododendron flowers grow in the deep shade of summer woods.

Rosebay Rhododendron often grow in thickets. Sometimes called hells in Ashe County vernacular.

Conifers

The five conifers tend to disappear into the overwhelming green of summer. Paul Gauguin, the post–Impressionist painter, once said, "A pound of green is greener than a half-pound of green." Ashe County is a hundred pounds of green during the summer. The conifers show off their green in winter when the landscape has turned to shades of brown, gray, and white. Unfortunately, the winter display of green has been greatly diminished by the mortal infestation of hemlock woolly adelgids in the eastern hemlocks. It is a sad sight to see the mighty hemlocks' gray trunks crumbling into the earth, dying off *en masse*. One of the most beautiful, majestic trees in the wild Ashe County landscape has almost been lost. The forest will absorb their decay and refill the holes in the canopy, but like the American Chestnut, another icon of the woods is disappearing.

Carolina Hemlock

On a brighter note, the Carolina Hemlock, the diminutive cousin of the Eastern Hemlock, is hanging on for dear life on some of the harshest exposures in the county. Their ecological niche is high elevation bluffs, crags, and outcrops where they put down roots in every fissure and seam in the rock. Their exposure to high wind, rime ice, and colder temperatures seems to be protecting them from the adelgid infestation. But in some of the lower-elevation stands of trees, the Carolina Hemlocks have been attacked and killed by the adelgids. They are definitely vulnerable to the adelgid, and even at higher elevation, global warming could impact their health in the future. They are an Ashe County treasure that live to be hundreds of years old, clinging to life on some of the county's most rarefied settings.

Carolina Hemlocks are at home on high elevation rocky outcrops on the Nature Conservancy's Bluff Mountain Nature Preserve.

The other three native evergreen trees of Ashe County are all pines. Thankfully, they are doing pretty well. A pine borer is doing some damage but so far does not appear to be a catastrophic threat.

White Pine

The White Pine is by far the most common of the three native pines. Not only do they grow in the wild, they are widely planted as timber trees and Christmas trees. They mature much faster into saw logs than any hardwood. White Pine can be harvested in thirty years when properly managed instead of the fifty years it takes for hardwoods. The lumber is widely used for paneling, cabinets, furniture, and cabin timbers. The wood is soft, light, easy to work, and has attractive grain and knots. The White Pine makes a decent Christmas tree when sheared and shaped, but isn't as popular as the

White Pine can grow into enormous trees with girths up to six feet in diameter and heights over a hundred feet. Adam Roberts and Sue Joyner are seen here standing in the shade of an old White Pine.

Fraser Fir. Its boughs, though, are made into garlands by the mile and shipped all over the country at Christmastime.

White Pine is used extensively in landscaping as shade trees, windbreaks, and privacy barriers. It is Ashe County's most commercially versatile tree and for all practical purposes is an industry unto itself.

A White Pine in full "bloom," though they are not flowering trees, about to loose its pollen to the wind.

Virginia Pine

The other two native pines are not as common nor as useful as White Pine. The Virginia Pine is a scraggly, messy tree and not used for much of anything. It doesn't grow big or straight enough to be saw timber, and only Charlie Brown would appreciate it as a Christmas tree. Virginia Pine does offer good wildlife cover, because it often grows into groves or thickets. All in all, in Ashe County—speak, the Virginia Pine is considered a "trash tree".

Table Mountain Pine

Table Mountain Pine is not common in Ashe County but is common in lower-elevation surrounding counties. They are scattered hither, thither and

Table Mountain Pine are attractive landscape trees but are not readily available in nurseries. They can be dug from the wild.

yon with no apparent rhyme or reason. Dry rocky ridge top or wet boggy bottom. When out by itself in a meadow, it is attractive and exotic-looking, almost Himalayan in appearance. Table Mountain Pine has interesting clusters of spherical, prickly cones that are bright green while they are growing. This tree would make a good focal point in a residential landscape, but as Table Mountain Pine is not available in the nursery industry, a seedling would have to be dug from the wild to plant in the yard.

Part II: Native Trees

The American Chestnut

The American Chestnut was the big daddy of the primeval hardwood forest in Ashe County until the late 1920s. The American Chestnut had been riding a wave of dominance for thousands of years. Something like one in four trees was a chestnut in their range. Then all of a sudden they died, killed by a virulent fungal blight delivered on the wind.

The American Chestnut has distinctive sawtooth leaves that are long and narrow with an extended point at the tip.

Chestnut stumps are all that are left of this once dominant tree of the southern Appalachian mountains. The author lends perspective.

Actually, by the time the chestnut blight blew into Ashe County, all of the valuable old growth trees had been cut down and hauled off by the Hassinger Lumber Company on the Virginia Creeper. What was left of the chestnut were young trees and trees that folks had saved for their own use. The blight finished them off. The Ashe County chestnuts had been wiped out in less than twenty years. The end. Sort of.

No one alive today will see their recovery. It will take hundreds of years for chestnuts to return to their former status if they become resistant to the blight. Mother Nature has her ways, and she is seldom in a hurry. There are some native chestnut trees popping up around Ashe County that are showing signs of blight resistance and have gotten old enough to flower and produce nuts. A very good sign but at this rate it could take a thousand years on their own to reestablish themselves. So, of course, humans have intervened and are trying to speed things up.

American Chestnut hulls must be handled with a gloved hand because they are like a ball of sharp needles.

Since the chestnut blight first appeared in 1904 in New York City, a cure has been sought; 113 years later, a cure is still being sought.

Four different strategies have emerged. The first two began early on, and the latter two more recently.

The chestnut blight did not kill every last tree, only 99.9 percent of them, which means one tenth of one percent were blight-resistant and did not die. The surviving trees were scattered over a wide range from Maine to Georgia, often in isolated, remote places unknown to anyone. So, the first cure strategy was to find blight resistant trees and breed them to each other. A commonsense approach, but not foolproof. Every tree carries genes of its predecessors, most of which were not blight-resistant. Therefore, the progeny of crossbred blight-resistant trees did not guarantee a blight-resistant offspring. Complicating things further is the time it takes a chestnut tree to mature to flowering age, produce nuts and show resistance to the blight.

In order to speed up identifying which trees are resistant, young trees are inoculated with the blight to see if they can fight it off. The trees that become sick are discarded, and the ones that stay healthy are grown out. When a resistant tree finally matures enough to flower and produce nuts, it is then cross-pollinated to other resistant trees, and its nuts are collected, planted, grown out, and tested for blight-resistance. The back-breeding of resistant native American Chestnut trees has been going on for generations, and for those folks wanting to see a pure strain of the American Chestnut return, assisting Mother Nature is the only way to go.

The second strategy is similar to the first but moving at a faster pace. It involves cross-breeding American Chestnut to blight-resistant Chinese Chestnut. Unfortunately, the American Chestnut and the Chinese Chestnut do not share the same size and form characteristics. The American Chestnut has been called "the Redwood of the East" because of its towering height and huge girth, whereas the Chinese Chestnut tends to be a low-branching, spreading tree under fifty feet tall.

The first-generation cross might make the offspring blight-resistant, but its form probably would not be that of an American Chestnut. The crossbred first generation would then be bred back to a pure American Chestnut and every generation from then on to pure American Chestnut so that ultimately the tall, straight, thick trunk form would be bred into subsequent generations. This is not a fast-track strategy either. Nothing is, but after many years of crossbred, back-bred chestnut trees, there are crosses that are $1/16$th Chinese Chestnut and $15/16$ths American Chestnut being planted in orchards and in the wild. For the purists, this isn't an American Chestnut, but it sure looks like one.

A more recent cure strategy is genetic modification. It is a controversial approach, because a gene from an entirely different kind of plant—wheat—is introduced to the American Chestnut genome. The controversy stems from messing with Mother Nature in a way dear old Mom would never want and in the long term could have unexpected results. Imagine chestnuts that tasted like whole wheat bread. Who knows. So far, the genetic modified chestnut trees have not been released to the public or the wild, but at some point, they probably will be.

Another recent strategy is to give the blight a blight, with obvious inherent risks. How will the chestnut-blight blight interact with other fungi and plants? Will it morph into an even bigger monster? That's a tricky question.

The American Chestnut has been called "the perfect tree." Before any human laid eyes on a chestnut tree, wildlife were dependent on them for food.

The number of organisms living on, in, and around chestnut trees were uncountable.

Chestnut trees bloom in early summer after the threat of late frost, so they bear nuts reliably every year, by the ton. Wildlife would gorge on the nuts in the fall to fatten up for winter. They were a vital part of the food chain for thousands of years.

When the first Native Americans arrived in Ashe County, they were following the food: buffalo, elk, deer, bear, and turkey, all chestnut feeders. The Europeans arrived looking for land, but they had to eat, too, and chestnuts were an important part of their diet. They also fed them to their livestock. In the fall, the settlers would let their hogs free-range to fatten up for slaughter. They also gathered the nuts to store for winter and to sell and trade.

The American Chestnut really was the perfect tree for the European settlers in Ashe County. Chestnut wood was strong, lightweight, rot-resistant, straight-grained and easy to work. An entire house could be built with chestnut wood, from the sills to the split-shake roofs. Rails split from ten-foot-long logs were stacked for fencing livestock and gardens. The wood was used for cooking fires and heat. The bark is high in tannins and used for tanning leather for clothing, harnesses, hinges, rope and whips. Without the American Chestnut, the European settlers would have been hard-pressed to survive and thrive in the wilderness and through the winter. There were no other substitutes for its nuts and wood.

The chestnut blight was considered by some to be the worst natural disaster in North America since the last Ice Age. Now it is nearly forgotten, because human needs are met globally, not locally. Someday the American Chestnut will flourish again in Ashe County, either on its own, or with the help of human intervention, but regrettably not in our early 21st century time. The folks working on saving and restoring the chestnut are selfless and altruistic knowing they will never see the end results of their work: stands of healthy one-hundred-foot tall, six-foot diameter American Chestnut trees, dropping mast by the ton.

The Beech Family

Life is a Beech if you are an Oak in Ashe County. White Oak, Northern Red Oak, and Chestnut Oak are the native oaks of the county, and all are members of the Beech family, which also includes their cousins, American Beech, American Chestnut, and Chinquapin. Their common denominator and distinguishing characteristic is that they all bear nuts and mast. (Mast are the nuts that fall to the ground.) Except for the Chinquapin, which is not as common or widespread, the rest of them are important members of the mixed hardwood forest in Ashe County.

More than any other trees, the beech family filled the niche vacated by the American Chestnut. By no means do they replace the reliable volume of mast the chestnut produced, but without the mast that the beech family does produce, wildlife would be threatened in Ashe County. The other nut-bearing trees in the county are the Pignut Hickory, Shagbark Hickory, Black Walnut, Butternut, and Buckeye, which mainly produce squirrel and chipmunk food. The beech family, with their soft-shelled, meaty nuts, provide food for a wider range of wildlife like bear, deer, raccoon, possum, coyote, skunk, turkey, crow, raven, grouse, and many other types of birds and rodents.

The acorns of the oaks are edible for humans too, but it takes some preparation to make them palatable. Acorns are high in tannins, which give the raw acorn a bitter, chalky flavor. To get rid of the tannin, the cap and the hull of the nut must be removed. The raw meat of the nut is then soaked in water overnight. (Chlorinated water will flavor the nut undesirably and should be avoided.) Pour off the water the next day and put the nuts in a cooking pot. Add fresh water until all of the nuts are floating. Put the pot on the stove and bring the water to a boil. When the water darkens, pour it off and add fresh water. Repeat this process until the water no longer darkens.

Then spread the nuts out on a cookie sheet and let them air dry. After they are dry, roast them in the oven. Be careful not to overcook; it makes them hard as a rock. Salt to taste. Sprinkling tamari sauce on them is good, too. Enjoy. Beech nuts, chestnuts, and chinquapins are good roasted as well and don't have to be soaked. Each member of the beech family in Ashe County is considered valuable, but some more than others.

Chinquapin

Chinquapin is valued mainly for its nuts. Of the beech family, the Chinquapin is the smallest tree and least common. Its nuts resemble an American Chestnut, only smaller but just as good to eat. A Chinquapin's form is more like a large, multistem shrub than a tree, which makes it an excellent residential nut tree. It does not take up a lot of space, has tasty, abundant nuts, and can be propagated by planting a raw, ripe nut in the fall. The trick is finding a Chinquapin from which to collect nuts. At one time they were a common tree in the Ashe County landscape but have mysteriously disappeared from the wild.

White Oak

If the American Chestnut was the big daddy of the Ashe County primeval forest, the White Oak was the granddaddy. It is by far the longest-lived tree in the county, but since the clear-cutting of the old growth forest, there probably are not any five-hundred-year-old white oaks still around. White Oaks can live beyond six hundred years in a favorable, protected exposure. It can reach heights over a hundred feet tall with a spread just as wide as it is tall. Unfortunately, big, old trees are considered a nuisance instead of a treasure and are often cut down or mangled by pollarding.

White Oak lumber is highly valued for its light blond color, hardness, strength, rot-resistance and unusual grain. Historically, it is used for just about anything wood is used for. Everything from furniture to foundation

On the following two pages: **White Oak: spring, summer, fall and winter. White Oak can live to be hundreds of years old and get to be as wide as they are tall when they grow out in the open.**

Part II: Native Trees

The Beech Family

Kim Hadley

Kim Hadley

sills, chair caning to roofing shingles, flooring to railroad ties, trailer beds to paneling, firewood to tool handles.

White Oak is not used much in residential landscaping, because they are slow growing, have messy mast and russet-colored fall foliage. It's a bad rap, though. Their mast feeds wildlife even in town and ultimately they make the best treehouse tree and swing tree in the county.

Northern Red Oak

The most common oak in Ashe County is the Northern Red Oak. It thrives from valley floor to the highest summits. Like the White Oak, its wood is a favorite for furniture and flooring. It polishes into a lustrous red, brown, blond fine-grained surface that appears to emit light from within.

In the open, Red Oak grows into a huge, spreading tree with a thick trunk, and in the forest, it reaches for the sky and can rise over one hundred feet tall. Unlike the White Oak, the Red Oak is not rot-resistant, which is an important consideration when determining where and how to use it. Red Oak is a long-burning firewood, but it must be put under roof to dry. If it is left out in the weather, it absorbs water like a sponge and will only smolder.

Like the other oaks, the Red Oak can produce heavy mast but not reliably every year. Of the three native oaks, the Red Oak is the most likely to be planted as a shade tree. It is the fastest grower and has attractive, dark red fall foliage.

Chestnut Oak

The Chestnut Oak is the least valued of the native oaks. It appears to have gotten its name from the shape of the leaves. The leaves resemble an American Chestnut leaf, only shorter and rounded on the edge of the leaf.

Chestnut Oak lumber resembles White Oak and is often passed off as White Oak in the lumber industry, but as Chestnut Oak wood ages, it darkens and more closely resembles American Chestnut. The wood is not rot-resistant. It is not as prized as the White or Red Oak, but like them, it is a major contributor of mast for wildlife. Chestnut Oak is rarely used as a shade

An old growth Northern Red Oak next to Highway 88 in Jefferson. Almost nine feet wide at its base, it's probably a relic of the original forest. The author poses with the tempting tire swing.

Northern Red Oak leaves have sharp points on their lobes and turn red in the fall.

tree in landscape planting but is often found in residential Ashe County landscapes where the natural forest is left intact.

American Beech

American Beech is laced throughout the mixed hardwood forest of Ashe County and is easily recognized by its smooth, gray white bark. Like its cousin the oaks, American Beech gets really big out in the open and tall in the forest. Unlike the oaks, it hangs on to dead leaves in winter and noisily rattles in the

A seedling Chestnut Oak. Its leaves are similar to an American Chestnut, but more rounded, not sawtoothed.

wind until spring. American Beech often grows in pure stands particularly on high-elevation ridges, and can live to be hundreds of years old. Its nuts are edible and small compared to chestnut and Chinquapin but are an important food source for wildlife, especially grouse and turkey.

Beech wood is not as prized as oak but is often used like oak. It is a heavy, hard, fibrous wood that is difficult to split for firewood and prone to rot. In the landscape, it is an attractive, slow-growing long lived tree that needs a lot of room to accommodate its eventual huge size.

A closeup of an emerging Beech leaf in spring. It's almost more colorful than their fall foliage.

Ashe County residents and wildlife would be hurting without the beech family. Not to say there is a current threat to them—there isn't. But as they filled the niche left vacant by the American Chestnut, there is not another group of trees out there that could fill the beech family role in the Ashe County forest.

American Beech in the fall are a mosaic of yellow, orange, green and brown against a blue sky.

American Beech clings to its leaves all winter, rattling in the wind until spring.

The Other Nut Trees

Black Walnut, Butternut, Pignut Hickory, Shagbark Hickory, and Buckeye are the other nut-bearing trees of Ashe County. Except for the Black Walnut, these trees basically produce squirrel food. Of course, other rodents, birds, insects and microbes feed off of their mast, too, and they are an important part of the Ashe County wild food chain.

Buckeye

The Buckeye nut is poisonous for humans and their livestock, but squirrels and other rodents seem to be immune to the poisonous nut. There are at least two nuts in every hull, and it has been said that one nut is edible and the other poisonous, but only squirrels can tell which is which. The Buckeye nuts' number one use by humans is as a good luck charm. Carrying a Buckeye nut in your pocket will supposedly bring you good luck.

Buckeye is the first tree in Ashe County to leaf out in the spring, and it is the first to shed its leaves in the fall. Buckeye is common in the mixed-hardwood forest, and mature trees can reach heights of eighty feet and diameters of four feet.

Lumber is rarely made from Buckeye, because it is soft and weak, which might explain why it is so common; no one cuts them down. Buckeye wood is used for carving, because it is easy to work and has unusual, irregular streaks of dark grain roaming around in the blond heartwood.

Buckeye makes an attractive but messy landscape tree. It is a showy, flowering tree with profuse clusters of yellow-white blooms all over the tree. On the messy end, it drops a ton of inedible hulls and nuts and big, brown leaves.

Buckeye nuts look like they have been polished after the hull pops them loose.

Buckeye flowers bloom in clusters all over the tree and make a beautiful but messy ornamental.

Buckeye leaves are the first to emerge in the spring and the first to turn in the late summer.

Black Walnut

The Black Walnut, on the other hand, is highly valued for its dark heartwood and its delicious, sweet nuts. Its wood is rot-resistant but seldom used outdoors. It is arguably the most popular furniture-grade wood in Ashe County, with Sugar Maple, Wild Cherry and White Oak close behind. Black Walnut wood isn't black like its name suggests, but instead varies from chocolate to reddish-brown with flecks and darts of dark chocolate to black grain. Its strength, light weight, dark color, and rot resistance make it desirable for gun stocks, too. Black Walnut grain is so tight and dense that hand grips can be checkered into the stock and the wood polished to a mirror finish. The Black Walnut has a spherical, large nut, bigger than a golf ball and smaller than a tennis ball and has a reputation as the ultimate ammunition for a two-inch diameter potato gun.

The hull of the Black Walnut is fleshy and aromatic and fairly easy to remove from the hard, inner nut after it has ripened and fallen from the tree. The aroma of the hull is sweet, astringent and fumy, and the juice of the hull stains everything it touches. To avoid the staining hull, a favorite technique (really) for removing the hull is to throw the fresh fallen nuts on the driveway and run over them with the car, truck or tractor until the hulls are knocked off. The hard, inner nuts are then gathered to crack open for the meat.

Black Walnut trees can take up a lot of space and should be planted out in the open away from buildings.

It is important the nuts are cracked soon after collecting them, while they are fresh. As in many foods, the fresher it is, the higher the quality. Also, if the nut shell is allowed to dry out, it becomes much more difficult to crack. If it can't be cracked right away, it should be stored in such a way as it can retain its moisture. A cool, damp root cellar is good, or it can be buried in moist sand, but not for too long. Fresher is better.

There are a number of ways to crack the nut of a Black Walnut tree. For small quantities, most folks hold the nut with a pair of pliers, pointed-end up against a hard surface like concrete or rock, and whack it with a hammer. There is some nuance to the whack—too hard and the nut explodes into little bitty pieces. Too light and the nut won't crack. It might take a few whacks to find the sweet spot.

Another method is to carve a shallow hole in a stump the approximate size and shape of the walnut, just deep enough so the walnut will stand on its own. Again, stand the pointed-end up, and whack it with a hammer. Pliers are easier to come by than nearby stumps, but this technique works really well, especially if the stump is a hard, rot-resistant Black Walnut.

For the more serious walnut producers, there are commercially produced walnut crackers available. If you are going to crack bushels of walnuts, this is the way to go. The nut is held tight by the cracker while a long-handled lever applies pressure to the nut and pops it open.

None of these methods are endgame. Most of the meat still has to be removed from the nut with a nut pick. Garnering a pound of Black Walnut meat is no small achievement, but well worth the effort. The Black Walnut meat is used in a myriad of recipes, from ice cream to salad dressing, to cakes, cookies and candy. Maple walnut scones fresh out of the oven are known to cause swoons and frissons.

The staining juices of the Black Walnut hull can be a pain to remove from hands and clothing, but the stain does have valuable practical applications. It can be used as a wood stain, fabric dye, and ink.

As a dye, depending on the strength or concentration, colors ranging from yellow to olive to brown can be obtained. It has been used for centuries to dye textiles, leather, wood and steel. In the fur trapping industry, steel traps were not only dyed with Black Walnut but also used to odorize the trap with a natural smell that hides human scent.

Black Walnut hulls have also been used for centuries to make ink for quills, paint brushes, and fountain pens. To make ink from walnuts, the hulls were boiled in water to extract the dye. The hulls were then removed, the dyed water filtered and brought to boil again. Much like making maple syrup, the water is boiled off until the concentration is thick and dark enough to be used as ink.

Black Walnut ink was and is still being used to make art. When used to draw or paint, the Black Walnut pigment is sepia, a popular medium to create moody landscapes and portraits.

The Black Walnut tree is not usually found growing in the middle of the mixed hardwood forest. Its niche is the edge of the forest or out in an open meadow. Unlike any other tree in Ashe County, the Black Walnut is allelopathic, which means it excretes toxic chemicals into the soil around it to suppress other trees or plants from encroaching. It is long lived, as in hundreds of years, and gets enormous with age.

In Ashe County, Black Walnut is not planted in orchards, because it takes generations to reach timber size, and the nuts are too difficult to commercially process. It is planted in residential landscapes for its shade and nuts but needs to be given plenty of room and planted well away from anything its nuts can bombard.

Butternut

There isn't much to say about the Butternut tree, other than it is native to Ashe County. It is not common, but where it occurs, it is often in multiples. Its nuts are edible but difficult to crack. Butternuts have a fleshy hull similar to Black Walnuts but not as big and not as round. It has been said by those who have a grove of Butternut trees and an abundance of nuts that the hullless nuts are so hard and rot-resistant that they can be used like gravel to repair or fill a pothole in a road.

Some people call the Butternut a White Walnut, but there is little comparison when it comes to the quality and utility of their nuts or wood. The Butternut wood is light brown and not as strong or durable as Black Walnut, but occasionally it is used for furniture and carving. As an ornamental or shade tree, Butternuts are very messy and undesirable.

Pignut Hickory and Shagbark Hickory

Pignut and Shagbark Hickory are both anchors of the mixed hardwood forest in Ashe County. Each can reach heights of over a hundred feet but have slender trunks compared to some of the other hardwoods of the same height.

Hickory nuts are edible and sweet but difficult to harvest in large quantities. A pound of hickory nut meat would take some serious nut-cracking to accomplish. Hickory nuts are a staple mast for rodents, which in turn are an important part of the food chain in Ashe County. Hawks, owls, ravens, foxes, bobcats, mink, raccoons, skunks, possums, and snakes all eat rodents that feed off hickory nuts. A squirrel perched on a limb of a tree munching on a hickory nut is easy picking for a hawk or owl.

Lumber made from hickory is used for flooring, cabinets, tool handles, and mallets. The heartwood is brown, and the sapwood is blonde, which

Newly leafed out Pignut Hickory with catkins (male flowers) hanging down. They are a common member of the mixed hardwood canopy.

Closeup of male Pignut flowers and a nut beginning to take shape.

Shagbark Hickory with vertical peeling bark makes them very difficult to climb.

makes for interesting contrast however it is used. The wood is heavy and hard but not rot-resistant and is susceptible to borers. It makes an excellent long-burning firewood but is heavy on the ash.

The Shagbark Hickory is distinctive for its loose strips of vertical bark peeling from the trunk. It is nearly impossible to shinny up for us humans and is rarely, if ever, used to build tree houses. The Pignut, on the other hand, has smooth bark—much more conducive to shinnying—and a better candidate for building a treehouse. Both Shagbarks and Pignuts drop their lower limbs as they mature in the forest and often don't have any limbs except in their crown.

Hickories are not as long lived as their counterparts in the mixed hardwood forest, so it is unusual to see a big old granddaddy hickory. They are not used in the landscape industry as an ornamental or a shade tree, but sometimes are left in the landscape when a lot is cleared in the woods. It is very undesirable to leave a hickory tree towering over a tin-roofed building.

The Maples

Red Maple

Red Maples are the first wild trees to bloom in Ashe County. When it isn't even spring, there they are casting off winter with a red glow in all that gray. Their blooms of course portend spring, but winter isn't done in mid–March Ashe County. It is uplifting, though, to see their red blooms defiantly poking out from under a blanket of wet snow.

Red Maple blooms are also the stop sign for the maple syrup season. Their swollen flower buds mark a change in the chemistry of the trees' sap, which indicates the sap is sweet no more, and it is time to pull the taps. Ashe County is not known as a maple syrup mecca, but every year from late January to mid–March, buckets hanging on maple trees collecting sap can be seen around the county. A few dozen industrious

Female Red Maple flowers. Red Maple trees are the first trees to bloom in Ashe County in the late winter. And see page 51.

Red Maple on the left, Sugar Maple on the right and Wild Cherry in the middle. They make for fall eye candy.

Male Red Maple flowers (above) are not as visible as the female flowers; they bloom together on the same tree. And see page 49.

souls with their makeshift evaporating pans and kettles are out there in their yards and sheds braving wind, rain, sleet, snow and dark of night, boiling and boiling and boiling and boiling the sap down to syrup and sugar. It takes about fifty to sixty gallons of sap to make a gallon of syrup. But anyone who has ever made their own maple syrup considers it worth the effort.

The maple syrup enthusiasts around the county gather every year on the third Saturday in March at the Florence Thomas Art School in downtown West Jefferson for the annual Florence Flapjack Fundraiser to compete, compare, and share their syrup. A blind taste-test is conducted by three non-syrup producers to judge three categories of syrup—light, medium and dark—with one best overall champion.

Red Maples are the most ecologically versatile of the maples. They thrive just about everywhere in Ashe County. Other common names for the Red

GEORGE REMBERT II

The winged seeds, called keys, of a Red Maple hang on stems until they are ripe and then blow away on the wind.

Maple include Swamp Maple and Soft Maple. They can be tapped for their sugar just like the Sugar Maple, but it takes a lot more sap to make a lot less syrup. They are best known for their brilliant fall color. Red Maples display every hue of red known to mankind, and along with their cousin maples, they are the pied pipers of the leaf-peepers every October. Ashe County coffers are annually filled with revenue thanks largely to the colorful maples.

Red Maples make a perfect shade and ornamental tree. They are fast-growing, disease-resistant trees, and they get huge. The nursery industry has developed a number of selected varieties with seductive names like October Glory, Red Sunset, and Autumn Flame. They are easy to transplant from the wild. In November, a small sapling can be dug bare-root, no root ball, and replanted. Phosphate should be added to the soil when transplanting to stimulate new root growth, and the tree will take off in the spring like it had never been moved.

Sugar Maple

Sugar Maple got its name for a good reason: its sap has a higher concentration of sugar than any other maple, but that isn't saying much. The concentration of sugar is usually less than 2 percent, which means that 98

Sugar Maple flowers are dainty but flower *en masse* giving the tree a chartreuse cast in the spring.

A huge 350-year-old Sugar Maple growing in the woods in a spot protected from the wind.

Sugar Maple leaves are just beginning to turn their fall color in front of a waterfall in the Clifton community.

percent is water and has to be boiled off. The process of getting to the sugar is totally evaporative, so it takes a while, even when using state-of-the-art equipment. The results are well worth it. Syrup made in Ashe County has a unique flavor and has been described by some maple syrup connoisseurs as the best they have ever had. (See page 219 for more on the maple syrup business.)

The five native maple trees in Ashe County are Sugar, Red, Black, Striped, and Mountain Maple. The Striped and Mountain Maples are typically understory trees in the mixed hardwood forest.

Black Maple

Black Maples are not common in Ashe County, but there are a few in the western part of the county along the Tennessee line. They, too, can be tapped for their sugar, and are sometimes called Black Sugar Maple. Like the Red Maple, their fall color can be spectacular crimson or even yellow.

Lumber made from Sugar Maple and Black Maple is prized for furniture, musical instruments, flooring, cabinets, and bowls. The wood is hard and heavy and can have unusual swirly grain. Red Maple is not as popular or desired as Sugar and Black Maple because of its soft, light wood, but it is used to build interior parts of furniture because of its light weight when kiln-dried.

Maples make up a significant portion of the mixed hardwood forest in Ashe County. Their fall foliage draws tens of thousands of visitors every October to see the show of color. There should be a name for such a phenomenon. How about the Ashe County fall pilgrimage?

Striped Maple

The Striped Maple is more common than the Mountain Maple and is also known as Goosefoot Maple, because the leaf resembles the shape of a goose foot. Its greenish bark is striated with vertical light-yellow and dark stripes, giving it a mysterious, enchanted quality, like something out of a children's storybook. Its large leaves, bigger than an adult's hand, are a deep emerald green in summer and turn light-yellow in the fall. Striped Maple is

Striped Maple bark comes by its name naturally and is a pretty ornamental tree year round.

Striped Maple flowers hang like bells attached to a stem, adding to their aura as a native ornament tree.

An emerging Striped Maple leaf responding to the change of seasons, unfolding to the light.

rarely used as a landscape tree, but it makes a beautiful specimen when it is. Its stem structure is similar to a Japanese Maple and can be pruned to that effect. Its unusual green, dark and yellow-striped bark add color and interest to a winter landscape.

Mountain Maple

Mountain Maples are not rare but are rarely seen or noticed. They tend to be loners and prefer rocky terrain, rock outcrops, and high elevation. They are not as much an understory tree as Striped Maple but are similar in size. Their spring blooms spike out the top of the tree in green-white cones with an orchid-like quality, and their leaves are sharply serrated and chartreuse in color, but are not as large as the Striped Maple's. They are often found in the company of Mountain Ash and Dwarf Willow at high elevation rocky ridges in complementary combinations.

The Birches

Yellow Birch

On the highest ridges of Ashe County, native Yellow Birch wrap their roots around boulders like they are holding onto prey. Others perch precariously on the edge of cliffs as if trained in grace by giant Bonsai masters, and some launch themselves into the tug-of-war between gravity and light, cantilevering themselves over an abyss. More commonly, though, Yellow Birch live along streams on humus-rich, rocky terrain. Their yellow to silver papery, horizontal-peeling bark is distinctive in the Ashe County woods. Often they will grow in pure stands, rising straight and tall. Children through the ages have shinnied their slender trunks to the tippy-top, kicking their legs out at the last possible moment of balance to ride

Kim Hadley

Yellow Birch's scrolled papery bark makes them easy to identify and makes a good fire starter for a campfire.

the arching tree back to the ground. Birches are maybe the origin of amusement park rides.

Black Birch

Black Birch is another tree that offers rides in the woods, but care must be taken identifying it. Black Birch closely resembles the European Cherry, a non-native tree introduced by European settlers that has escaped into the wild throughout Ashe County. The European Cherry's black, red, or yellow cherries are choice and yummy, so they are a welcome invader, but it is important to distinguish Black Birch from it if one is a swinger of birches. Whereas Black and Yellow Birch will give you a safe, thrilling ride, European Cherry will snap in two halfway down and land you on your back with your wind knocked out or worse.

Robbie Franklin contemplating a gravity-defying Black Birch, circa 2001. Growing in the bouldery terrain near the summit of the Creston Peak.

A Black Birch seems to be attempting to swallow a boulder and has been working on it a long time.

Black Birch is also known as Sweet Birch for its wintergreen aroma when the bark is peeled back from the stem. In the days before toothbrushes, Sweet Birch twigs were shredded or pointed at one end to clean teeth and freshen breath.

Like maples, the sap of Black Birches can be boiled down to make syrup or candy, but the flavor is not the same as their aroma. Instead of a wintergreen flavor, the syrup tastes more like a mix of licorice, horehound, and molasses. Not as desirable as maple syrup, but good eating nonetheless, it takes twice as much birch sap as maple sap to make half as much syrup. Before the days of food and drug regulations, birch syrup was mixed half and half with high octane moonshine and sold as an elixir. If it didn't cure your malady, it certainly made you feel better about your condition.

Birch wood is blonde in color and easy to work, which makes it desirable for building furniture, musical instruments, and carving. It is also used as veneer, particularly in finish-grade plywood.

In the landscape, Yellow Birch is an attractive but messy tree. In the spring, it drops catkins and tends to drop leaves throughout the growing season, especially during a drought. Black Birch does the same but is rarely used or offered as landscape trees.

Blue Beech

Blue Beech and Hophornbeam are two lesser-known members of the birch family in Ashe County. Both are understory trees. Blue Beech is more commonly known as Ironwood, because its wood is so heavy and dense that it sinks instead of floating in water. Its smooth, steel-gray bark appears to be stretched tight over sinewy tendons and muscles. It is usually found near streams, springs, and bogs, but occasionally it occurs high and dry. Its trunk branch multistems from the ground, and if Blue Beech has enough room, will branch as wide as it is tall. Blue Beech is rarely used as a landscape plant, but it can be an interesting addition to a pondscape.

Blue Beech with ripening seeds, and dark green foliage make for an attractive landscape tree but are seldom used as such.

Blue Beech trunks have a muscular appearance and are also called Ironwood but are a member of the Birch family of trees.

Hophornbeam

The Hophornbeam is common in Ashe County, but it is probably the most anonymous, least-known tree in the woods. It is usually a single-stem tree in the understory and has light-brown shaggy bark. The fruit or seeds closely resemble hops hanging from its twigs but are not the least bit showy.

Hophornbeam trunks rarely get thicker than fifteen inches in diameter and are a common tree in the mixed hardwood forest understory.

Hophornbeam seeds waiting to release. They germinate readily and sometimes grow in thickets.

Like the Blue Beech, its wood is heavy, dense, and tight-grained, which makes it desirable for tool handles. Dry Hophornbeam wood is excellent for firewood, too, particularly for wood cook stoves.

    The birch family is a widely-distributed mainstay of the Ashe County hardwood forest. Their yellow fall color is an integral part of the leaf-peeper show, but swingers of birches are in decline and may be relegated to the "good old days."

The Magnolias

None of the three native magnolias in Ashe County is called a magnolia. All of them are common as crows, and one of them is highly valued for its lumber, bark, and honey made from its flowers. Their names are Tulip Tree, Cucumber, and Wahoo.

Tulip Tree

Tulip Tree is also known as Tulip Poplar and Yellow Poplar but isn't a poplar at all. It's a member of the magnolia family. Its lyrical botanical name, *Liriodendron tulipifera*, doesn't exactly clear up its identity, but if you look in a tree identification book, you will find it under magnolia or *Magnoliaceae*. They are one of Ashe County's most common and valuable trees.

Tulip Tree gets its name from the shape and look of its flower. Though not as bright and showy as a tulip flower, Tulip Tree flowers are beautiful in their own way. Instead of brilliantly-colored outer flower petals, the Tulip Tree flower has green outer petals with a small splash of orange that blends into the greenery of the leaves. But on the inside or throat of the flower they are bright orange and yellow. They also have a fruity fragrance. Their aroma is sweet and pungent, and on a still, humid day, their scent wafts deliciously in the air.

Bees work Tulip Tree blooms in a frenzy and make thick, dark honey from the pollen. When Tulip Trees are in full bloom the buzzing of the bees gathering pollen sounds like the trees have a motor running.

Tulip Trees are prolific seed-bearers. In the fall after the leaves have dropped, the wind releases their winged seeds by the thousands, often filling the air like a cloud of whirling insects. Tulip Trees and maples are the trees quickest to reseed cleared land. Their seeds can fly a long way on the wind,

Tulip Tree flowers are beautiful but usually are not close enough to the ground to admire—but bees swarm to them to make a dark honey from their pollen.

and they germinate readily. Tulip Trees are fast-growers, dominating reclaimed land in pure stands of straight, very tall trees. They are considered a hardwood, but they are a soft, heavy wood when freshly cut. Tulip Trees are full of water, but when they dry out, the wood becomes lightweight and hard. Fresh-sawn Tulip Tree lumber can be strikingly colorful for a short while, showing off streaks of cerulean, ultramarine, purple, cyan and even scarlet, but the colors fade quickly when exposed to the air. Tulip Trees are the rainbow trout of wood.

The bark of saw timber–sized Tulip Trees is used for siding on cabins and is just as valuable as the lumber. The bark is harvested during the growing season, or as some folks say, "when the sap is up." Care is taken in removing the bark in sections that are as large as possible before being cut up into flattened shingles to dry. Care is also taken to keep the bark clean, so the bark is usually removed from the tree where it falls. Dragging the logs through dirt and mud soils the bark and makes it unusable. Boards sawn from Tulip Trees are blonde to light brown when fresh-cut, but the grain and knots darken to chocolate with age and make for beautiful paneling and cabinets.

Unfinished Tulip Tree wood makes good siding for outbuildings as long as the wood can dry out after getting wet. It is no good for continuous exposure to moisture or dampness and will quickly rot if it stays wet.

Historically, old growth Tulip Trees were gigantic, in the same category as American Chestnut, often reaching heights of 150 feet and diameters of up to ten feet. There are few places where old growth stands of Tulip Trees remain untouched, but the most famous is here in North Carolina at the Joyce Kilmer Memorial Forest near Bryson City. There you can walk through a relic primeval forest and get a glimpse of what these mountains looked like before the short-sighted greedy white boys arrived.

Cucumber and Wahoo don't get as big as the Tulip Tree and are not as commercially valuable. Even so, they are both an important part of the Ashe County mixed hardwood forest.

Wahoo

The Wahoo is also known as Mountain Magnolia and Fraser Magnolia. It is the prettiest of the three native magnolias, with its large, white flowers

Wahoo has a large fragrant flower that appears while the new leaves are unfolding in the spring and is used as an ornamental shade tree.

Wahoo leaves are the biggest in the Ashe County woods and grow in a whorl, which make them easy to identify.

and long whorled leaves. In late summer, its seed pod is shiny crimson and resembles a peeled pomegranate. In the woods, its flowers and fruits are difficult to see, because they are in the top of the tree. But as a landscape ornamental tree standing alone in the open, Wahoo blooms top to bottom. It is one of Ashe County's most beautiful flowering, fragrant trees. Unfortunately, it is not readily available in the nursery industry but can be transplanted bare-root from the wild in the fall as a seedling.

Cucumber Tree

The Cucumber Tree is the pigpen of the magnolias. First the leaf bud's outer covering falls off, littering the ground. Then the flower bud's external layer peels off and falls to the ground. After that, the tulip-sized flowers fall apart and fly everywhere. But it's not done yet. Next, the seed pods rain down

A ripe Cucumber Tree seed pod. Most of the seed pods fall off the tree before they ripen and make a mess but the ones that do ripen have brilliant colors.

like fat, green caterpillars, and then its large, brown fall leaves shed almost all at once. There is one fun, redeeming quality to its leaf litter. Some of the fall leaves fold themselves into the shape of a boat's keel, and if they land just right or are placed just right on a pond, they will sail around for a while at the whim of the wind. Lumber sawn from the trunk of a Cucumber Tree dries very lightweight but isn't valued for anything in particular, so the logs don't bring much at the mill.

The magnolias add another layer to the rich diversity of the mixed hardwood forest in Ashe County and are healthy, hardy trees in what has been a stressed-out forest over the last hundred years.

The River Trees

The New River meanders through Ashe County like a snake seeking the route of least resistance, slipping by trees and boulders. Any of the trees of Ashe County can line the banks of the rivers and streams, but there are three kinds of trees that need wet feet. They are Black Willow, Balsam Poplar, and Sycamore.

Weeping Willow are not native to Ashe County, but they have been successfully planted around the county. Fortunately, they haven't gone wild, invasive, or dominant, because mature Weeping Willows take up a lot of space and might displace the native Black Willows.

Black Willow

The Black Willow doesn't get as big as Weeping Willow but is substantial just the same, reaching heights up to fifty feet. More often, it is in the twenty- to thirty-foot range. Black Willows are almost never straight stemmed. Their trunks are dark, almost black, and grow canted, angular, and multistemmed with olive green foliage pom-pommed at the terminus of their limbs. They are common along the rivers and streams, but are never high and dry. Black Willow can grow so irregular and cantilevered that they look like they have been tended by a Japanese gardener, especially when fog is drifting through them.

Black Willow are rarely used in landscaping. Most folks prefer the Weeping Willow, but they have almost identical foliage on a totally different, just as interesting, form.

Black Willow are a common sight along all of Ashe County's streams and rivers and add an unusual form to the landscape.

Balsam Poplar

The Balsam Poplar is Ashe County's only native poplar. Local folks call them Bam Bud or bom-a-gilly or Balm of Gilead. Like the Black Willow, Balsam Poplar needs plenty of water, and unlike the Black Willow, they grow straight and tall. In the spring when their leaf buds begin to open, they are aromatic, and their piney scent can be detected hundreds of yards away.

Historically, the sticky buds of the Balsam Poplar were picked by mountain folks and sold to local medicinal plant buyers. An old-time buyer said he had no idea what kind of medicine was made from them, he just bought and sold them to make money. No one is buying medicinal plants in Ashe County anymore. It is another practice relegated to "Remember when?" But there is a nursery in Ashe County growing and selling medicinal transplants for home use that can be purchased at the Ashe County Farmers Market.

A few Bom-a-Gilly line the bank of the north fork of the New River off Ed Little Road in the Clifton community.

Balsam Poplar wood is heavy and full of water when green but dries to a very light weight. Boards sawn from it look like chipboard, because the wood is so coarse and fibrous. Lumber from Balsam Poplar is weak and soft and rarely used for much of anything, not even firewood.

Most of the time, Balsam Poplar trees are singular or in twos or threes, but sometimes will grow in pure stands. They make an attractive landscape tree for a wet spot, and their fragrance is a rare treat.

Sycamore

Sycamore. What a name. What does it mean? Where did it come from? Dictionaries say the word has multiple origins. Middle English: *Sicamour*. Middle French: *Sicamor*. Latin: *Sycomorous*. And Hebrew: *Shiqmah*. The word's origins indicates that Sycamore was a geographically widespread, well known tree, but there is no explanation for what the word means. The Sycamores of Ashe County are no relation to the Sycamores of Europe and the Middle East but somehow ended up with the same name. So let's just call its origin "Middle Ashe" and not worry about what it means.

Sycamore is also known as American Plane Tree, Buttonwood, and Mud Maple. Mud Maple is the only colloquial name that makes any sense, as Sycamore leaves resemble maple leaves, and they grow on bottomland, which can get muddy at times.

Sycamore trees can grow really big both in height and girth. A good example of how big they can get is the Sycamore on Old Field Creek Road in front of the River House Bed and Breakfast Inn. It is a multistem giant with a ten-foot diameter trunk and a massive, spreading crown.

Sycamores are distinctive for their bright, white bark in the top half of the tree. A mature Sycamore growing along the river is a landscape painter's delight, particularly in crepuscular light. Even better, walk along the river after a winter snow on a full moon, and Sycamores become grand ethereal sculptures looming in the night.

Sycamores are rarely logged in Ashe County, because their wood isn't valued for anything in particular. But historically they were logged. During the clear-cutting of the old growth forest a hundred years ago, everything was cut.

A Sycamore towers over the north fork of the New River near Creston. They grow all along the waterways of Ashe County.

The giant Sycamore in front of the River House Inn, circa 2001, is a magnificent old growth tree with a multistem base over ten feet wide. The author provides perspective.

Sycamore are occasionally used in landscaping. They grow fast and make a good shade tree. Beware, though: they get an unsightly blight on their new growth in spring that makes them look like they are dying, but they recover once the weather warms up.

In addition to their pastoral beauty, Black Willow, Balsam Poplar, and Sycamore are all important erosion controllers. Their roots reach out in all directions from the trunk, holding themselves up and the bank around them in place. The shade their crowns provide in summer helps keep the water cool and offers a haven from the sun for fish, wildlife, and wee critters. They are to the river what clouds are to a rainforest.

The Cherries

Black Cherry, Choke Cherry, and Pin Cherry are the native cherries of Ashe County. Unfortunately, none of them produce edible cherries for us humans, and worse, two of the three are poisonous. The Black Cherry, famous for its salmon-colored wood, has toxic cherries, foliage, twigs, and bark, and probably kills more livestock than any other poisonous plant in Ashe County. Fortunately, the cherries are not toxic to birds and wildlife, and annually, cherries produce abundant food for wildlife.

The Pin Cherry is not poisonous but is not palatable and has very little flesh on the pit. The edible cherries of Ashe County, Black Heart, Red Heart, and Honey Heart, appear to grow wild but are all introduced cherries that have escaped into the wild.

Black Cherry

The Black Cherry is also known as Wild Cherry and is prized for its wood, which is used for furniture, cabinets, paneling, flooring, and crafts. It also makes good firewood, grilling wood, and smoking wood. Black Cherry wood chips soaked in apple juice overnight are excellent for a smoldering fire in a covered cooker with a side of pork.

Black Cherry is a common tree in the mixed hardwood forest of Ashe County, whereas the Chokecherry and Pin Cherry prefer the edge of woods, fencerows, meadows, and logged over land. Birds and wildlife spread their profusion of seeds, and cherries are often the first trees to colonize neglected land.

A profusion of Wild Cherry blooms is a common sight in spring and they grow tiny cherries later (which aren't edible).

Pin Cherry

The Pin Cherry is a short lived tree, usually dying out after only twenty or thirty years, but it is one of Mother Nature's best erosion controllers, particularly on clear-cut logging sites. They readily take hold on disturbed, torn-up soil and produce seeds at an early age, which further adds to reclaiming the land. Its bark is a distinctive, lustrous, smooth mahogany-red and is valued by children in the know who have pocket knives to cut and peel the bark for making miniature canoes to paddle on the rivers of their imagination. Pin Cherries tend to grow in thickets, and when they bloom in spring, put on a display *en masse* of white flowers as if covered in snow.

Choke Cherry

Choke Cherries are poisonous raw, earning their name, but can be boiled into edibility. They have more flesh on the pit than Pin Cherries and

A Choke Cherry coming into full bloom. It produces a cherry that can be juiced and made into a jam with lots of sugar.

are used to make jelly by squeezing the juice through a sieve, adding pectin, and lots of sugar. Like the Black Cherry, Choke Cherry bark, foliage, and twigs are poisonous and should be removed from livestock pastures and pens. They are common in Ashe County along the edge of woods, open fields, and fencerows. Farmers must be diligent in removing them from fencerows where birds are constantly planting them.

The native cherries of Ashe County are not considered good landscaping trees, because their fruit is messy and poisonous. They do attract birds, but that only adds to their messiness.

Serviceberry

When the Serviceberry trees bloom in Ashe County, you know for sure that spring has arrived. It will snow and frost some more, but the ground will not freeze again.

During the late eighteenth and early nineteenth centuries, the climate was much colder in Ashe County than it is now. Back then when someone died during the winter, there was no way to hand-dig a grave for burial. The ground might as well have been concrete it was frozen so solid. So the bodies of the dead had to be stored away until the ground thawed. The Serviceberry bloom signaled that the thaw had arrived and that it was time to dig graves, hold services, and bury the dead.

There are many trees with two or three common names, but few have six. Shad, Shad Blow, Shadbush, Shadberry, Sarvis, and Saskatoon are all colloquial monikers for Serviceberry, depending on what part of the country you are in. Here in Ashe County, the colloquial name is "Sarvis," which sounds a lot like "service" and probably originated from the dialect of the Scotch-Irish settlers.

"Shad" comes directly from the shad fish. The shad spawn like salmon by swimming up streams and rivers in huge schools at the same time that the Serviceberry blooms, which alerts fisherman to keep an eye on the water and their nets ready.

"Saskatoon" probably comes from early settlers trying to pronounce the Native American name for Serviceberry and segued into English first orally and ultimately into the written word. A good name, "Saskatoon," but not a name used for Serviceberry in Ashe County.

Serviceberry gets the other half of its name from the edible fruit it produces. The reddish-purple fruit is sweet when fully ripe but almost never gets ripe, because it is a favorite food of goldfinches and cedar waxwings. A flock

Serviceberry is the second native tree to bloom in early spring just after the Red Maple, and portends the true arrival of spring.

of either bird will descend on a Serviceberry tree in a feeding frenzy well before the fruit is ripe and clean out every berry.

Serviceberry is an excellent, beautiful landscape tree. Typically, it grows in a multistem clump with smooth, steel gray bark. Its white to pale pink blooms come before the leaves appear in late March or early April depending on the weather. It is a small tree that fits nicely into a residential landscape and usually can be found at local nurseries.

In the wild, Serviceberry seldom grows in multiples but is common and pops out singularly and noticeably when it blooms like a scattering of lights coming on in the gray of early spring.

Serviceberry make excellent ornamental landscape trees with their heavy spring bloom and summer berries.

Sassafras

Sassafras is best known for its root beer–like aroma and flavor, and there is a reason for that. In the days before synthetic aromas and flavors, Sassafras root was used to flavor root beer. Unfortunately, Sassafras is suspected of

Sassafras can be used as an ornamental tree and can be dug from the wild when it has no leaves.

Sassafras trees grow county-wide and are often in coppices. The three different shaped leaves are in fall display.

This Sassafras tree was planted in the yard of Linda Osborne in Creston by her father. She didn't like it and cut it down—but it grew back and turned out to be beautiful.

being a carcinogenic plant and is no longer used to flavor beverages or food. The sarsaparilla drink was also flavored with Sassafras which likewise was dropped as an ingredient after discovering it was a cancer-causing agent. It's too bad, because Sassafras is common and easy to grow in Ashe County. At one time, Sassafras roots were valuable for farmers and root collectors, and were shipped all over the world as a flavoring agent and medicinal remedy.

Sassafras trees often grow in thickets, which seems to stunt their size, but when they are out in the open and singular, they can grow into a large tree. Sassafras are easy to identify when they have leaves. For one, the leaves are aromatic when crushed, and second, it is the only tree in Ashe County that has three different-shaped leaves on the same tree, a characteristic which is known scientifically as an anisophyllous tree.

Sassafras is an attractive flowering tree, but its yellow flowers are small and not strikingly visible. Its black fruit attracts birds in the summer, and its orange, yellow, and red fall foliage is brilliant, but oddly it is seldom used as a landscape tree.

Sassafras wood is aromatic and bug-resistant, but like the American Holly it seldom gets big enough to make lumber from it.

According to the dictionary, the origin of the word "sassafras" is Spanish, but it has the ring of Native American to it. Either way, it comes off the tongue right up there with Saskatoon, sarsaparilla and suffering succotash.

Staghorn Sumac

Staghorn Sumac gets its novel name from the appearance of the tree when it has no leaves. The trunk and forked limbs resemble the antlers of a stag elk.

Characteristically, Staghorn Sumac grow in dense patches similar to blackberry patches. It is an exotic-looking tree in summer, with pink-stemmed compound leaves. Some leaves have more than twenty pointed

Staghorn Sumac is an exotic-looking tree year round with its unusual leaflets and its brilliant color in fall.

Thickets of Staghorn Sumac thrive along the roadside throughout Ashe County but can be invasive when planted in a yard.

leaflets to a single stem, and its greenish-yellow cluster flowers poke out the top of the tree's canopy. It looks and grows like a tree from the jungle. In the fall, its leaves turn bright crimson, and its flowers morph into a cockscomb of a burgundy seed pod. Its teardrop-shaped seed pod remains after the leaves drop and can be harvested to make a citrusy herbal tea.

The wood of a Staghorn Sumac has a soft, pithy center and can easily be hollowed out. Children in the know make smoking pipes from them, hollowing out one end of a short piece and adding a goldenrod stem. Then they gather cigarette butts and glean the leftover tobacco to smoke. If there aren't any cigarette butts lying around, they pick rabbit tobacco and smoke that.

Before there were any commercial spouts available for tapping maple trees, farmers would make their own taps using hollowed out Staghorn

Sumac stems. The spouts only lasted one season, but they were free for the picking.

    Staghorn Sumac is a beautiful landscape tree but needs to be contained or it will take over. It can be grown in a large ceramic or wooden planter, in an island surrounded by concrete, or in brick or stone planters that are cemented together. Think bamboo when planting Staghorn Sumac. It is worth the effort and is one of the showiest native trees in Ashe County.

Ash

Mountain Ash and American White Ash are not related to each other genetically, but they share a common last name and both are deciduous trees thriving in the mixed hardwood forest of Ashe County. The genus and species of Mountain Ash is *Sorbus americana*, and the American White Ash is *Fraxinus americana* which, coincidentally, means they share a botanical last name as well. Yet, the two are disparate members of the mixed hardwood forest.

American White Ash

American White Ash grows into a very large, tall tree and is found throughout the county. Mountain Ash is found mostly at high elevation, above 4,000 feet, and only gets up to about thirty feet tall. Above 4,500 feet, Mountain Ash becomes more shrub-like.

White Ash is valuable for its lumber, which is light brown to blonde, straight-grained, and strong. It is used for furniture, baseball bats, tool handles, interior trim, and cabinets.

White Ash never grows in pure stands

A White Ash about to bloom appears as a mass of tightly clustered flower pods about to burst onto the scene.

BETTY REMBERT

but is evenly mixed with the other hardwoods throughout the county. It makes a handsome, fast-growing shade tree with few, if any, pest problems (but looming like a dark cloud to the north is the emerald ash borer). Out in the open, its crown can get as wide as the tree gets tall, and in the woods, it reaches for the sky and rises to more than a hundred feet tall.

Mountain Ash

Mountain Ash wood has no commercial value, but as an ornamental landscape tree it is popular and valuable. It is a showy, flowering tree with compound leaves similar to the Staghorn Sumac, but with red leaf stems instead of pink. The flowers are white clusters all over the tree that then turn into clusters of bright orange to red berries in the fall. If the birds and bears don't find the fruit, the berries can hang on after the leaves drop well into the winter.

The Mountain Ash and the American White Ash fill niches not as noticeable or visible as say the oaks, maples, or pines, but nonetheless, they are both good examples of just how rich and diverse the mixed hardwood forest is in Ashe County.

Mountain Ash fruit add color to the landscape after the leaves drop in the fall. The tree is an attractive ornamental for the home landscape.

Linden

The Linden tree is common in Ashe County and is also known as Basswood and Bee Tree. Like the White Ash, it doesn't grow in pure stands and is scattered among the mixed hardwoods of the county. It usually doesn't get as thick and tall as oak, Tulip Tree, or Sugar Maple, but sometimes does under special circumstances, seen in the Linden off Brushy Fork Road near the Tennessee line (see next page). This Linden tree shared a fenced-in lot with generations of bulls and traded shade for fertilizer (manure). It grew to

Linden blooms attract bees to their pollen and honey made from their pollen makes one of the tastiest treats ever.

Linden trees usually don't get as big as this one up on Brushy Fork but this one grew out in the open for a long time. Jimmy Savely is examining the dying old trunk (circa 2001).

six feet in diameter and a hundred feet tall. Mature Linden trees ordinarily grow to three feet in diameter and seventy-five feet tall.

The Linden tree is called Bee Tree for a good reason. Honey made by bees collecting pollen from its flowers is considered some of the best-tasting honey there is. It's right up there with Sourwood and Tupelo but much rarer. It is almost impossible to get pure Linden honey, since the trees are so widely scattered. Its flavor is similar to a very sweet orange and is so good it is surprising no one has planted an orchard of Linden trees just for the honey.

Why Linden is also known as Basswood is anyone's guess. Of all the trees in the county, it is the lightest weight wood when dry. The wood is nearly white in color and has almost no visible grain. Linden is soft and easy to work but not high in demand.

Sprouts growing around the base of the trunk make good walking sticks because of their light weight, but they aren't very strong and easily break. When making walking sticks from Linden sprouts, de-bark them, let them dry out for a few days and make more than one stick, so there will be a back-up when the first one breaks.

Tupelo or "Black Gum"

Tupelo trees are few and far between in Ashe County. It is easiest to spot in the fall when its leaves shout red and yellow, but its fall color is very similar to some Red and Sugar Maples and tends to blend into the landscape instead of stand out.

Tupelo is also known as Black Gum and probably gets its name from its distinguishing but inconspicuous small, black fruit. Its flowers and fruit are

A mature Tupelo appears to be an explosion of woody growth. They grow into a very large tree. Scattered about the county, they almost never grow in pure stands.

Tupelo or "Black Gum"

This towering Black Gum was left during the last logging, dwarfing the new growth forest around it.

more visible on young trees than on mature trees, because Tupelo drops its lower limbs as it grows tall—up to a hundred feet—and the flowers and fruit disappear into the canopy.

The Tupelo makes a beautiful shade tree but doesn't spread nearly as wide as White Oak or Sugar Maple. Its crimson and canary fall color is a spectacle, particularly when it stands alone. Tupelo is not available at Ashe County nurseries but can be ordered from nursery catalogs.

Tupelo wood is of little commercial value in the county, because there are so few of them. Firewood cut from Tupelo is nearly impossible to split by hand, but it is a hard, dense wood that makes for a lasting fire.

Honey from the Tupelo is highly prized. It is so sweet that Irish balladeer Van Morrison wrote a song about Tupelo honey using it as a metaphor to describe the sweetness of his woman: "She's as sweet as Tupelo honey." Unfortunately, there are not enough Tupelos around to make pure Tupelo honey in Ashe County.

Hawthorn

Hawthorn just barely qualifies as a tree. Occasionally it will get over twenty feet tall, which is the height that must be reached to be called a tree, but more often it is shorter.

Hawthorn is a thorny, prickly tangle of a tree. It prefers open fields, meadows, and the edge of woods but can be found in the understory of larger trees if the canopy isn't too overgrown. It often forms impenetrable thickets and is invasive on pasture land.

Betty Rembert

Hawthorn make an outstanding flowering ornamental with a flourish of flowers and fruit every year.

Hawthorn have serious thorns and bright red fruit and can be an invasive tree in pastures and meadows.

Hawthorn is a member of the rose family, which speaks to its thorns, and it is a showy bloomer with white flowers filling its crown in spring. It is often used as an ornamental tree, not only for its flowers, but for its fruit and fall color as well. Hawthorn's fruit or hips are abundant bright red, staying on the tree well into winter, and its leaves turn orange and red in the fall.

Hawthorn hips can be harvested and dried to make a medicinal herbal tea. Supposedly good for the heart, the hips also make excellent slingshot ammunition, because they are round, hard, and don't weigh very much.

The very worst impenetrable thicket in Ashe County occurs when the introduced, invasive Multiflora Rose comes up in a Hawthorn thicket. The only way to deal with this combination of plants is to bulldoze them into a pile and burn them.

Hawthorn wood is hard and heavy, but its multitude of long thorns protect it from being sought out. Better to leave Hawthorn alone unless it's in your way.

Sourwood

Sourwood grows wild near the eastern Continental Divide in Ashe County, especially around the Blue Ridge Parkway, and is planted as an ornamental tree over the rest of the county. Sourwood is considered one of the prettiest trees in the landscape, right up there with flowering Dogwood, but it is not as readily available at nurseries as Dogwood. Small Sourwood seedlings can be transplanted bare root from the wild after the leaves drop in the fall.

Sourwood blooms after the summer solstice, so it never gets burned by late frost. Its blooms are numerous drooping fans of tiny bell-shaped flowers hanging from stems. Sourwood is a member of the Heath family, which includes Rhododendron, Mountain Laurel, Blueberry, and Dog Hobble, which are all shrubs except for the Rosebay Rhododendron.

Sourwood seeds cascade from the tips of its branches in colorful fans against the backdrop of their red fall color.

Kelly Clampitt

A lone Sourwood tree is an eye catcher and a beautiful speciman for planting in the yard.

Honey made from sourwood is considered to be the best there is in this neck of the woods and is remarkable not only for its flavor but also its color. In its pure form, Sourwood honey is nearly clear but rare to come by. More often it is pale yellow, because some of the bees found something else blooming along the way. It brings a higher price than other honey and stirs up more conversation about honey than any other tree. At the Ashe County Farmers Market, a number of vendors sell honey, and there is always an old-timer or two who remember when their granddaddies made Sourwood honey clear as moonshine.

The Sourwood tree can get fairly big, up to forty and even fifty feet in a perfect setting such as someone's yard where it gets fertilized every year. But typically, it stays under forty feet in the wild and has a caliper under a foot. As a landscape ornament tree, it is attractive year-round, and as a wild tree it adds another splash of red in the leaf-peeper season.

The wood of Sourwood is not sought out for any particular use these days, but legend has it that Sourwood made good sled runners once upon a time.

Black/Yellow Locust

Black and Yellow Locust are the same tree, and the only native tree in Ashe County that is a member of the legume family of plants and trees. In these pages, it will be referred to as Yellow Locust for clarity. Other familial legumes are peas and beans, which are famous for adding nitrogen to the soil. If you compare the flowers of a Yellow Locust to a pole bean flower, they are almost identical.

In recent years, Yellow Locust has been afflicted by a nasty little bug called a Leaf Miner. It eats the leaves from the inside out and turns them from green to brown by midsummer. It doesn't kill the tree but weakens it, making it more vulnerable to attacks from other insects and fungi, which will eventually kill it.

Locust is a fast-growing tree when it first sprouts, sometimes putting out eight to ten feet of new growth in a single

BETTY REMBERT

Locust flowers are a tasty edible treat but beware of the thorns lurking along the stems waiting to poke intruders.

growing season. It spreads by root runners as well as seed and is aggressively invasive in pastures and meadows. Yellow Locust is also at home in the mixed hardwood forest where it can reach a hundred feet tall, competing for sunshine in the top of the forest canopy, particularly on north- and northwest-facing slopes. Out in the open, it doesn't get as tall and has a thicker trunk.

Before the leaf miner blight arrived in Ashe County, Yellow Locust was a highly valued wood for a number of uses, but no more. The blight, in combination with shelf fungi and carpenter ants, has ruined the formerly rot-resistant hardwood. Now words like punky and dodey (rotten) are used to describe the condition of the wood, which makes it unusable for everything but firewood.

In the past, the heartwood of Yellow Locust made the best, longest-lasting fence posts, sills, timber, and decking. Sometimes the bark was left on a fence post, and if it was set green, the fence post would sprout new growth, take root, and grow into a tree again. Fence posts made of locust heartwood can last over fifty years.

Yellow Locust is the best firewood in the county. It is like burning coal

A heavy Locust bloom portends a good Locust honey yield but mature Locust trees are in decline, another victim of a type of blight.

but a lot cleaner. A woodstove stoked with locust before bedtime will still be going strong at dawn. Unfortunately, locust firewood, once as common as people who are afraid of snakes, is getting hard to find. Another attribute of locust firewood is that it will readily burn green. Of course, it has more creosote green than cured, but if you start running out of firewood in the middle of winter, it is reassuring to know that green locust will bail you out.

Honey made from locust flowers rivals Sourwood honey for taste and clarity, but unlike Sourwood, locust doesn't bloom consistently every year. When it does bloom, it is usually a heavy bloom, and the bees crank out some exceptional honey.

Another important thing to know about Yellow Locust is that it has wicked thorns similar to those of tame rose bushes. A puncture from a locust thorn is poisonous and can cause swelling and extreme debilitating soreness. Handle locust with care and heavy gloves.

Yellow Locust is rarely planted as a landscape tree, but it used to be. The leaf miner blight makes locust unsightly in late summer and destroys its yellow fall color. There are some big, old Yellow Locust trees at the Ashe County Park along the Frisbee golf course that show off their beauty and value in the Ashe County landscape despite their many issues.

Witch Hazel

Witch Hazel is another tree that just barely qualifies as a tree. It does get taller than twenty feet at times, but more often not. Its growth habit is typically out, not up. So, if you stood the out up, it could reach twenty feet or more.

Witch Hazel is a common understory tree in the mixed hardwood forest, but it is also commonly found along creek banks out in the open and along the edge of fields.

It is a medicinal tree. The distilled extract made from its leaves, bark,

Witch Hazel is one of the most unusual flowering trees in Ashe County. They bloom late in the year when nothing else is blooming.

The hull of the Witch Hazel is about to launch a bead seed out into the landscape away from the parent tree.

and twigs is commercially available at drugstores and is used to soothe insect bites, nettle sting, mild burns, sunburn, and rash.

Before the botanical buyers of local herbs and roots went out of business in Ashe County, Witch Hazel leaves were a staple of wild herb collectors. The leaves were collected by stripping them from the stem with a gloved hand and stuffing them into a tote sack. When the tote sack filled up, the leaves were dumped out on a sheet or quilt laid out on the ground. The leaves were piled as high as possible, then contained by pulling the four corners of the sheet together and tying a knot at the top. The bundle was unwieldy but lightweight, and three or four of them would fill a pick-up bed. The green leaves could then be hauled directly to market, or if a space like a barn loft was available, the leaves could be spread out to dry. Selling dried leaves was more profitable but more time-consuming. No one got rich gathering Witch Hazel leaves or any other herbs and roots, but it did supplement farm income. And anyone who has ever farmed anything knows every dollar counts.

Wild Witch Hazel is an unusual choice for a domestic landscape garden but a good one. Its spidery yellow blooms appear after most or all of the leaves are gone in the fall. Not much else is blooming in Ashe County in October and November, so Witch Hazel pretty much has the stage to itself. Its flowers are small and dainty, so it isn't a big show but a delicate delight against a backdrop of gray, brown, and sometimes white. Witch Hazel branches are often cantilevered at eye level, so the flowers can be admired up close. At that time of year, some will sparkle with tiny ice crystals on their petals.

Historically, Witch Hazel branches are a favored material to dowse or divine for underground water. This is done by cutting a Y-shaped branch from the tree and walking around with the bottom of the Y pointing ahead. If the branch detects water below, the tip of the branch will dip towards the spot, letting the dowser know where to dig or bore. These days, dowsing is a bit of a lost art, but it is still performed by those in the know.

Witch Hazel is also known as Bead Wood. The seeds of the tree are housed in a hull, and after a year of clinging to a branch, the seeds are ejected from the hull in all directions. The tiny, black seeds resemble a bead and may actually be used as beads by resourceful folks.

Witch Hazel limbs reach out for the space around them to float their scallop shell–shaped leaves in summer. Turning yellow gold in the fall, its frilly, jeweled flowers are one of many of natural wonders in Ashe County.

Flowering Dogwood

Dogwood is an unlikely name for such an iconic, revered, beautiful tree. There are breeds of dogs that are iconic, revered, and beautiful, but none of them are called wood dogs. For whatever reason, the adopted state flower of North Carolina's stuck with its moniker, though it is not a dog of a tree. Worse and even ironic, Flowering Dogwood's botanical name is *Cornus florida*, not *Cornus north carolina*.

Dogwood flower buds form the year before they bloom and their fall foliage adds to the colorful fall show in Ashe County.

Flowering Dogwood blooms heavily around the county every spring to the delight of everyone.

Flowering Dogwood is the full common name, not just dogwood, because there are other dogwood varieties in Ashe County. "Flowering Dogwood" distinguishes it from Alternate-Leaved Dogwood and Silky Dogwood, which are both shrubs, not trees. But when someone refers to "dogwood," everyone understands they mean Flowering Dogwood and not the other two. With that in mind, another question arises. Why is the Flowering Dogwood the state flower and not the state tree?

Long Leaf Pine is the state tree of North Carolina, but there isn't a native Long Leaf Pine west of Interstate 77. Sure, some have been planted west of I-77, but none of them found their way on their own. Long Leaf Pine are native to the coastal plain, and whoever designated them the state tree had probably never been west of Tarboro. And, by the way, Long Leaf Pines do not have leaves, they have needles. It is a travesty and an insult to the western half of the state that the Long Leaf Pine is the state tree. The Carolinas got divided the wrong way. It should be West Carolina and East Carolina.

On the other hand, no other tree flourishes so magnanimously statewide as the Flowering Dogwood, with the emphasis on "tree." The only other flowering plant that flourishes statewide and is as well-known as dogwood,

Flowering Dogwood

A lone Dogwood stands up to the test of winter and the ferocious wind.

though infamously, is poison ivy. Flowering Dogwood should be the state tree and poison ivy the state flower, which metaphorically speaking characterizes the state of North Carolina more accurately.

Before 1980, dogwood used to thrive everywhere in Ashe County. Then an airborne fungal blight called anthracnose arrived and started killing them in the woods. The blight was lethal in the shade of the understory of the hardwoods where there is more moisture and less evaporation. Dogwoods at the edge of the woods and out in the open have been able to resist the blight, because they can dry out in the sun and breeze. Fortunately, the blight has not wiped out the dogwood in Ashe County. It continues to put on a major floral display every spring and a crimson leaf show in the fall. It also produces bright red berries that migrating flocks of birds like Evening Grosbeak and Cedar Waxwing feed off as they head south.

Dogwood blooms at the height of spring in a wave of white flowers. Its large white flower petals are actually a kind of leaf, and the flower is in the center at the base of the white leaves. Its flowers occur at the tip of its twigs and can bloom in such profusion that they obscure the rest of the tree. No other native tree in the county has blooms so full and bright.

Flowering Dogwood is the number one flowering tree planted in residential Ashe County landscapes. It is easy to transplant from the wild in the fall when seedlings can be dug up bare root for transplanting. It is also readily available at nurseries and garden centers in larger sizes, both balled and burlapped, and in pots. The nursery industry has developed varieties of Flowering Dogwood that have pink and red blooms, but those do not occur in the wild. The native dogwood can be used for root stock to graft colorful varieties onto.

The wood of Flowering Dogwood is tight-grained, hard, and heavy. It is occasionally used for tool handles and chisel mallets. It rarely gets big enough for saw timber. Cured dogwood makes excellent firewood for the fireplace or woodstoves, because it burns slow and long with lasting coals.

Flowering Dogwood is a cherished tree in Ashe County and across the entire state of North Carolina. It is a feel-good tree when it blooms in spring. Flowering Dogwood brightens the day and lifts the spirit.

Bringing the Train to Todd

Up Horse Creek
Men and horses.
Some good, some bad.
Good blood
Bad blood.
Good boss
Bad boss.
Dynamite and pick
Blasting the rock
Leveling the grade
Following the creek
Bringing the train
To Todd.

Young fools
Old fools
Young hearts
Old farts
Pushin' and pullin'
Draggin' and totin'
Smokin' and drinkin'
Girls back home
Minx on the road
Sheep in the barn
Knives hid away
Bringing the train
To Todd.

Saw mill
Rail head
Cross-cut saw
Double bit axe
Cut them trees
Ever last one.
Good liquor
Bad liquor
Bear meat
And possum.
Missing moma
Bringing the train
To Todd.

Groundhog
And ramps
Fetch a meal
Hot and cold
Rain and sun
Snow and ice
Mud and blood
Ford the river
Logs and steel
Timbers and saws,
Don't miss Paw
Bringing the train
To Todd.

No train no more
Just the poor
Hassinger lumber
Run out a trees.
Ripped up the tracks
Got the hell
Out of Ashe
Found a new stand a
Trees to trash
Some wallets are full
Most are empty
Taking the train
From Todd.

Part III: Introduced Trees

Introduction

Ashe County is a treasure-trove of native trees, but as of 2017, there are likely more introduced varieties of trees than native. Some introduced trees have escaped into the wild but haven't become invasive, which is a good thing, because non-native invasive trees and plants can wreak havoc in the wild: think Multiflora Rose and Kudzu, both of which can and do overrun a landscape.

When Kudzu gets going, it can completely dominate and cover trees, shrubs, buildings, power poles, power lines, fields, and streams. If left unchecked, the trees it covers die. Multiflora Rose is just as nasty and invasive a plant as Kudzu but more insidious with its armor of thorns. It can take over a fence line, fill a pasture, or climb up into trees. Goats will eat it, but cows and horses won't. Its seeds are spread by birds and mammals, and it can grow anywhere but deep shade.

Both of these introduced, escaped, invasive plants are a threat to the trees of Ashe County. Little, if anything, is being done countywide to control Multiflora Rose and Kudzu, and as a result, they are spoiling more and more land. Once they get going, they become nearly impossible to control. A good example of runaway Kudzu and the mess it can make is on Highway 88 west of Warrensville on Baker Hill around Blue Ridge Elementary School.

Non-native introduced ornamental trees are a wonderful addition to the beauty and scenery of the county. Trees like Colorado Blue Spruce, Crimson King Norway Maple, Weeping Willow, Mimosa, Japanese Maple, Dawn Redwood, Cripps Cypress, Fringe Tree, Alaskan Cedar, Hybrid Poplar, Atlantic Cedar, Leyland Cypress, Flowering Cherry, Purple Leaf Plum, Weeping Cherry, Styrax, Arborvitae, Chinese Fir, Norway Spruce, Catawba Tree, Bald Cypress, Ashe Leaf Maple, Yellow Wood, Carolina Silver Bell, Fernspray Cypress, Black Pine, European Cherry, Boulevard Cypress, Alanthus, Lemon

Thread Cypress, Golden Raintree, Hinoki Cypress, Scotch Pine, Paulownia, Golden Chain Tree, Flowering Crabapple, Peach, Full Moon Maple, Apple, Chinese Chestnut, Pear, Nellie Stevens Holly, European Birch, Asian Birch, Paperbark Maple, Purple Beech, Silver Maple, Sawtooth Oak, Big Tooth Aspen, Slippery Elm, Concolor Fir, Deodara Cedar, Fraser Fir, Kousa Dogwood, River Birch, Ginkgo, Asian Spruce, White Spruce, Redbud, Smoke Tree, Cottonwood, Lombardy Poplar, and Bradford Pear, to name some, are planted around the county with success.

The climate in Ashe County varies quite a bit with change in elevation. The lower elevation southern and eastern part of the county is known as the Florida of Ashe County. The higher elevation northern and western part of the county is known as that Alaska of Ashe County. Some of the non-native trees mentioned do better in one part of the county than the other. (If global warming continues at its current pace, Christmas tree farms will be replaced with citrus groves, and a drive to the beach will get a lot shorter.)

Trees are dearly loved and affectionately appreciated by many folks in Ashe County, as is evident by the trees planted in yards and along driveways and roads. The towns of Jefferson, West Jefferson, and Lansing all plant and maintain trees along their roads and in their parks. Unfortunately, the village of Warrensville has not followed suit and has treeless parking lots along its short main drag. Trees not only add beauty and shade to a community; they also offer historical perspective. The town of West Jefferson just celebrated its centennial in 2015, and for the first time in its one-hundred-year history, planted trees down Jefferson Avenue and 2nd Street. Before that, the lone tree planted on Jefferson Avenue downtown was the iconic Catawba tree in front of the historic Bantam Chef and Colvard Oil Company. It has solitarily anchored the entire street for generations with its huge crown and has become a landmark of the town.

Sugar Maple trees have been planted along Highway 221 in Jefferson, which is an excellent choice for a street tree. They are long lived native trees, have brilliant color in the fall, and require no maintenance. Unfortunately, someone decided they needed to be maintained and had them pollarded. Pollarding is a type of pruning widely used to keep trees from growing tall by whacking the top out of the tree. It is a ghastly, unhealthy approach to pruning a tree. Some trees, like Bradford Pear, can handle it and are even improved by pollarding. A good example is the row of pollarded Bradford Pears on Jefferson Avenue in front of Leviton Manufacturing Company. They get cut back every year or two to keep them from growing into the power lines. Sugar Maples can't take pollarding and often die as a result, which is evidenced by the loss of trees along 221.

Pollarding trees in Ashe County is a common practice and has resulted in some very unsightly, damaged trees. This expensive butchering of trees could be avoided completely with foresight. When a tree is planted in the landscape, give it the room it needs to mature. If a lot is being cleared for the construction of a building, and there are existing trees, thin them out and give them room to mature well away from the building. Another way to avoid pollarding is to plant trees that don't get big and tall.

Pollarding old trees is almost always fatal. If not immediately, then over time as the exposed wounds are attacked by fungi and begin to rot. The most dramatic death of an old tree by pollarding occurred in Warrensville in 2015. A healthy two-hundred-and-fifty-year white oak was killed. The old tree was

Pollarding old trees is a bad idea because they usually die right away or over a period of a few years.

Pollarded Bradford Pears actually benefit from getting whacked, it keeps them from falling apart in the wind, ice and snow.

a much-photographed landmark in the community. The late Joe Robinson of Creston told the story of stopping his horse-drawn wagon at this tree in the early twentieth century on his way to Jefferson from Creston. It was a huge tree of a hundred and fifty years then. In the shade of the old tree, he would take a break and hook an extra horse to the wagon to help pull the load over Baker Hill.

There is also a legend about the old oak being used as a hanging tree during the Civil War, but there is no factual evidence to corroborate the story. The point being, the grand old White Oak spanned a period of history from the Native American genocide to the election of an African American president. Trees can offer a profound historical perspective when allowed to live out their natural lives.

Take the old oak stump in front of the Arts Council building in West Jefferson. After it died from a lightning strike, it was cut down to the ground. Most folks know counting the rings on a stump will reveal its age, because a tree adds a ring every year of its life. This old oak's life began in 1747, two hundred and seventy years ago. Its life probably began in the woods and likely wasn't felled during the clear-cut a hundred years ago, because a property owner left it for shade near a house or barn. West Jefferson was founded in 1915 when the oak was already huge and nearly a hundred and seventy years old.

In Jefferson near the intersection of Highway 88 and Old 16, there is a Northern Red Oak that is almost nine feet in diameter at its base (see page 33). It is likely one of the oldest living trees in Ashe County. A few years back, Highway 88 was being widened, and the old oak was in the way and was going to be destroyed. Fortunately, a long time Jeffersonian, David Worth, said hold your 'dozers and saved the ancient oak. Old trees are important landmarks. Historically, they have been used to designate a property line or a corner of a boundary. Some of the biggest, oldest trees in the county remain for this purpose. Other old trees are saved by their footprint being on a property line and are shared property, not to be messed with.

Ashe County folks generally appreciate trees but not passionately. The public schools have not made it a point to teach children their trees, plants, and animals. It is an enigmatic problem considering we live among the trees, plants, and animals and not the other way around. They were here first, and they are not anonymous. They have identities and live and die just like us. We are their neighbors. We share this spot on the planet with them. We should get to know them.

Knowledge is truth and understanding. Knowledge of the immediate environment and ecology is comforting. Acknowledging nature and its vast complexity is a sensory buffet, and there is no better way to appreciate the marvels of nature than to introduce yourself to the trees of Ashe County.

Ornamental Trees

The early Scotch Irish settlers of Ashe County brought with them seeds of fruiting trees to plant on their homesteads. There were no native edible fruiting trees to write home about so they had to bring seeds or trade for them. There is no evidence that John Chapman, better known as Johnny Appleseed, ever visited Ashe County but seeds from the tens of thousands of apple seeds he introduced to the Appalachian frontier might have indirectly made their way here during the latter part of the eighteenth century and the early part of the nineteenth century. Apples and cherries were likely the first trees introduced to the county but they were not introduced for their edible

Downtown Jefferson circa 1900 with three rows of Cherry Trees funneling the traffic (photographer unknown).

fruit or aesthetic value as much as for making alcoholic beverages. Scotch Irish settlers were known for their skill making hard cider, apple jack and brandy and even more well known for their consumption of their beverages.

It is impossible to know what it was like for the first settlers arriving in the Ashe County wilderness. The whole of the county was old growth forest. Trees had to be cut down and cleared to open the ground to the sun for gardens, crops, meadows and pastures. The settlers were farmers not hunter gatherers like their Native American predecessors. Cutting down a six to eight foot diameter tree with nothing but an axe must have taken days to accomplish. Then the real work begins, processing the massive tree into workable material for constructing a house, barn, shed, tools and fencing. Everything was done with hand tools, a maul, wedges, broad axe, adze, draw knife, mallet and froe. And what to do about the stumps? An old timer that farmed in the early part of the twentieth century said they would cut down the trees, fence the cleared area with split rails, turn the cattle in and wait twenty years for the stumps to rot. Those homesteaders were tough and patient.

The log homes they built for themselves just barely kept winter at bay. In addition to hand making every part of the house, the sills, joists, flooring, door and window jambs, doors, shutters (they had no glass), rafters, roofing, shelves and furniture, they had to stack a chimney from stone and chink it with mud and moss. During the winter snow would blow through every crack and hole and settle like finely sifted flour on their furniture and floors. Most of the heat went up the chimney. The only way to stay warm enough to sleep at night was to nip some applejack and snuggle up against the hearth with a quilt. To keep food from freezing they would bury it and dig it up as needed. Water had to be dipped from a spring in the yard or from a hole chopped through the ice in a creek and carried in a pail back to the house. A latrine was nothing more than a hole in the ground with frozen snow covered poles to sit on. There were no roads or grocery stores. If you had to go somewhere you walked. Most folks were too poor to own a horse. Instead they had oxen to plow, drag and milk. There was nowhere to buy spirits so they made their own. Booze was the balm for weary souls living on the edge and apples and cherries were the source.

Ornamental trees came later. They followed closely on the heels of law and order and town building. Post office, jail, town hall, court house, school, church, general store, mill, McDonalds, forge, stable, doctors office. Houses and roads were built. Trees were planted. Shade trees were the first air conditioners. Oaks and maples transplanted from the woods were favorite yard trees and European cherries were popular too. In 1900 there were three rows of cherry trees lining main street in Jefferson, a row down either side and a row down the middle. There wasn't any pavement or curb so the trees funneled the slow moving, sparse traffic. The cherry trees bloomed pretty in spring above the mud and ruts of the road, then dropped their petals in a snowflake like flourish hiding the mud for a few days. In late June the cherries would ripen and delight the taste buds of passersby. Children would climb to the tops of the trees where the cherries hung in bunches, stuffing their bellies while fending off blue jays and crows. Unfortunately cherry trees are not long lived like oak and maple so those cherry trees lining main street died out by the time the road was paved and cars and trucks arrived replacing oxen, wagons and horses. Sugar maples replaced the cherries in some places on main street but road widening left some buildings too close to the road with no room for trees and we lost the tree lined street.

 The best time to plant a tree is twenty-five years ago. Even then you are getting a late start. Most trees are infants at twenty-five. It is one of those disparities in nature that is confounding. Why is it dogs live such short lives and trees such long ones? It is not fair. Mother nature doesn't seem to have a penchant for fairness, she does what she pleases.

Ginkgo

There are some trees that do mature at twenty-five years, like fruit trees, but most trees are just getting started. Take the ginkgo (also sometimes spelled gingko) tree for example. They can live well over a thousand years and are just a suckling babe at twenty-five. It has been said ginkgo trees take five hundred years to grow, five hundred years to live and five hundred years to die. Not only are they a long lived tree, they have the oldest lineage of any tree on earth dating back to the dinosaurs. At one time ginkgo trees were spread worldwide in all temperate ancient forests including North America, but ultimately disappeared in the wild. Their fossilized leaves have been found in North America but they mysteriously died out long before humans wended their way to Ashe County. Their wild native range must have overlapped with human time in Asia because someone took a shine to them and started propagating them before they disappeared in the wild.

Ginkgo trees are dioecious, having a male and a female. The female ginkgo bears nuts that are edible but noxious to harvest. When the outer hull of the nut splits open they are ripe and redolent of rotten eggs. Without the hull the nut cleans up to a pure white and is considered a delicacy in Asia but they have not caught on in the western hemisphere. Someone young should plant a grove of female ginkgo trees along with a few male pollinators here in the county to sell at the Ashe County Farmers Market. Maybe they would catch on like the Christmas trees have and you would only have to plant new trees every thousand years. Live like you are going to die tomorrow, farm like you're going to live forever.

Ginkgo trees are not commonly planted in Ashe County but there are a few nice specimens around. Since the female trees bear stinky nuts, male trees are preferred for planting as a landscape ornamental. To ensure the gender of the tree make sure to buy a grafted male instead of a seed grown tree.

Ginkgo leaves have a unique fan shape with a notch in the middle of the outer edge of the leaf.

Trees are often planted as memorials for deceased loved ones and the long lived ginkgo is considered the ultimate memorial tree. A ginkgo was planted as a memorial tree in the lawn in the middle of the paved walking trail at Ashe Services for Aging on Ray Taylor Road. Though the tree is small now, someday it will be over a hundred feet tall and a hundred feet wide if it is left alone to mature. It was planted with that intention and was given plenty of room to grow. It is impossible to anticipate what changes might occur over the next thousand years in front of the Ashe Services for Aging. The buildings will come and go every hundred years or so but hopefully the ginkgo tree will become an icon of age and a remembrance of the 21st century as it begins to die in 3016.

Ginkgo trees are one of the most beautiful trees on earth. Their unusual fan shaped leaves are unique in the tree world. Another common name for the ginkgo is maiden hair tree.

Another interesting characteristic of a ginkgo tree is the shedding of

Ginkgo trees are not commonly planted around Ashe County but they make a hardy, handsome and huge shade tree. Often used as a memorial, this one (about 25 feet tall) was planted to honor Ashe County artist Lissy Mahler.

their leaves in the fall. Their leaves all fall at about the same time or over just a couple of days. As a result the ground underneath the tree is encircled by glowing gold leaves for a few days which in turn uplight the stark gray trunk as if uplighting a sculpture. It is a particularly nice effect during twilight.

Ginkgo trees can be purchased at some nurseries. Make sure to get a grafted male tree unless you are interested in having nuts which come with a smelly booby prize. Beware too, they are susceptible to late spring freezes which burns their new growth but not to worry, they always recover. As they mature they become more cold hardy and are less vulnerable to late freezes.

Ginkgo trees are the mother of all big beautiful shade trees. Everyone who has room for one should plant one. You will only be disappointed by how slowly they take off and grow but look at it this way, what else can you plant or build that might last a thousand years!

Dawn Redwood

While you are out shopping for a ginkgo tree to plant you might want to keep an eye out for another dinosaur tree called the Dawn Redwood. This ancient tree was thought to be extinct and was only known from fossils until 1941 when one was discovered at a remote Chinese temple. At the time, the discovery was considered the botanical find of the twentieth century. But in 1994 another extinct dinosaur tree called the Wollemia Pine turned up in

The bark of the Dawn Redwood peels, furrows and scales from the swollen trunk in a way that herbs can take hold in the coarse cavities.

Dawn Redwood trees get really big faster than most any other tree. This one was planted from a rooted cutting in 1983. Wheeler Munroe gives perspective.

Australia and stole some of the Dawn Redwood's thunder. They were both amazing discoveries in the tree lovers world and both of these trees have been propagated and made available in the nursery industry. Unfortunately the Wollemia Pine is not hardy in Ashe County and cannot survive here. The Dawn Redwood though is very cold hardy and does well in all parts of the county.

Dawn Redwoods are deciduous conifers unlike native Ashe County conifers which are all evergreen. They are a fast growing tree, especially if planted near water or in a wet spot. They do fine high and dry but at a slower growth rate. Their crown grows into a perfect cone as if they have been topiaryed. The base or butt of the trunk swells massively in disproportion to their height similar to a Bald Cypress. They are often mistaken for a Bald Cypress because of their bell bottom shaped trunk, conical crown and similar needles. Both do well in Ashe County but neither are widely planted. More on Bald Cypress later.

Dawn Redwood do not take up as much room as ginkgo trees but they get big a lot faster which is a consideration in locating them. They are a very attractive unusual tree and make a great focal point in a landscape design. Their late fall orange foliage is visually striking because they are the last tree to show color after all the other trees have dropped their leaves. Their spring and summer foliage is fern-like in both color and form adding to their dinosaurness. They are open branched, graceful trees with the tips of their limbs and twigs drooping toward the ground. Standing beneath a mature Dawn Redwood there is a sense or mood created by their unusual ancient look that seems to say, "Have a seat. Take your shoes off. Set a spell."

Bald Cypress

The Dawn Redwood and the Bald Cypress are cousins but they look more like fraternal twins. The Bald Cypress is better known than the Dawn Redwood because they are native to the coastal plain of North Carolina. Their natural territory is the black water country where the highways are built on elevated berms so the traffic can zoom by on the way to the beach. They are better known as bagged cypress mulch or cross sections of their trunks made into clocks or coffee tables. Bald Cypress trees are too closely associated with swamps, snapping turtles, water moccasins and alligators to have warm fuzzy feelings about them for most folks. In spite of that they are spectacular ancient trees.

The Bald Cypress has the distinction of being the longest lived native tree east of the Mississippi River. They are right up there with the ginkgo tree in longevity. Along the Black River in the Three Sisters Swamp in Sampson County there is a Bald Cypress tree named Old Methuselah whose first year on earth was A.D. 364. We're talking 1,653 years ago. That is 603,000 sunrises. That is 1,130 years before Columbus discovered tens of millions of people living in the Americas. That is 1541 years before the first Ashe County court house was built. That is 1652 years before trees were planted down Jefferson Avenue in West Jefferson. And Old Methuselah is still going strong.

Bald Cypress make a beautiful, eye catching landscape tree and are as cold hardy and vigorous in the tempestuous mountains as they are by the balmy sea, a little known fact even in the sylvan savvy culture of Ashe County. Like Dawn Redwood they prefer wetscapes but will make it okay high and dry. They are a perfect complement to a pond or stream. There are very few

Opposite: **Bald Cypress are rarely planted in Ashe County. Tim and Judith Winecoff planted this one thinking it was a Dawn Redwood.**

of them planted in Ashe County which is a two part enigma: since you rarely see them, they do not come to mind in a mountain landscape and nobody asks for them at local nurseries so nurseries do not carry them. Now that you know Bald Cypress do just fine in Ashe County, pick one up at a nursery on the coast next time you are there. When you set one out make sure to give it plenty of room. They get really big in a few hundred years.

The Spruces

Red Spruce

There are no native spruce trees in Ashe County but there is one variety that used to be here and are still hanging on nearby at higher elevations. They are the Red Spruce. They can be found on Elk Knob just across the county line in Watauga County and on Mount Rogers and Whitetop Mountain in southwest Virginia. The Red Spruce is a relic of the boreal forest living at the highest elevations, a mile or more above sea level, in the southern Appalachian mountains. Though they do not occur in the wild in Ashe County they can be planted with success at lower elevations but seldom are. They are an attractive, long lived, open branched evergreen tree that have not found favor in the landscape nursery business. The Red Spruce is less popular than the ornamental spruces but that does not mean it is not worthy of our attention. They are a beautiful, dark green. It may take some doing to find one to plant in your landscape since most local nurseries do not grow them but they probably could be found on the Internet. For those tenacious, savvy conifer folks, Red Spruce is a diamond in the rough and a great addition to any Ashe County landscape garden.

Colorado Blue Spruce

The Colorado Blue Spruce is the most popular spruce planted in Ashe County and rightfully so. They are magnificent trees in their prime. A stunning bright light of a tree. They draw the eye to their beauty whether they are a focal point in the landscape or not. Unfortunately they are not long lived; a fungal blight called Blue Spruce needle cast slowly defoliates them

Betty Rembert

and eventually kills them. The first signs of needle cast appear on the bottom branches and the interior of the tree and works its way up to the top. The healthy life span of a Blue Spruce, before they become unsightly, is about twenty years. They are still used and grown extensively in Ashe County but plan accordingly. Plant them more like a shrub, anticipating twenty to twenty-five years before replacement.

The number of different Blue Spruce varieties is a long list and because they are so popular, new varieties are being developed in the nursery industry all the time.

The sales pitch is always the same, "a new bluer variety, bluer than ever before." The nursery industry is splitting hairs. The Thompson Spruce is a variety that has been around for a long time and is considered the classic Cadillac of the Blue Spruces. They are more conical and upright than the rest of the Blue Spruces and their vivid light blue color is what everyone likes and expects from a Blue Spruce. They are fast growing once they are established, putting out fifteen to twenty inches of new growth a year and they can be planted in a tighter space because they are more upright and less spreading. The Thompson Blue Spruce is the Eiffel Tower of Blue Spruces.

Norway Spruce

The Norway Spruce is just as popular as the Colorado Spruce but for a different reason. They are a beautiful tree planted alone in the landscape but they are more commonly used as wind breaks or visual barriers, planted *en masse* or in rows. They are faster growing than other spruce varieties and their thick, dark green boughs grow together as one, *à la* "e pluribus unum." As a mature free standing tree they have a Japanese pagoda look with their upturned limbs and their drooping foliage and cones. They can reach heights over a hundred feet and their mature size is commonly overlooked at their planting but it is wise to remember Norway Spruces grow into giant trees.

Opposite: Thompson Blue Spruce are a popular landscape ornamental tree. Unfortunately they are being attacked by a fungal blight that is hard to control.

A great Old Norway Spruce towers over the now deserted homeplace of the late Joe Robinson. The tree was planted in 1900 to honor the birth of a baby.

Joe Robinson standing in front of his homeplace by a Sugar Maple on left and Old Norway Spruce on right (circa 2001; the author at extreme left).

White Spruce

White Spruce are not as well known as Colorado or Norway Spruce but they are commonly used by landscapers in Ashe County. Instead of field growing white spruce and selling them balled and burlapped, nurseries grow them in containers and sell them at smaller sizes which are not as expensive as B&B. They transplant well and are fast growing. They are long lived trees with no pest problems of any kind. Even deer will not eat them. Since they are usually set out in the landscape at smaller sizes they are relegated to the fringe areas and the hole plugging spots instead of being the stars of the landscape. They are not there to outshine or compete, instead they subdue the empty spots in the landscape that require a quiet presence. No one asks for their name. No one says "Wow, what kind of tree is that?" White Spruce are the backup singers of the landscape.

Oriental Spruce

There is one more spruce worth mentioning. There are a gazillion varieties of spruce and half a gazillion of them do well in Ashe County, but the Oriental Spruce does particularly well here. They are an extraordinarily mag-damnificent tree. This is a spruce to seek out as a legacy tree. You will not live long enough to see what it will become but your gift to the landscape will be admired and enjoyed for a long time to come. They are slow growing but eventually grow into a very tall tree, over a hundred feet. They are a specimen type tree and a focal point. With that in mind they are best set out by themselves in a meadow or field. There are different varieties of Oriental Spruce available such as the "Gowdy" or the "Aurea" and they are very attractive too but the *Picea orientalis* (its botanical name) is the one to get. Their needles are short, dark green and hug the stem. They should be left unpruned unless they try to grow more than one leader and the extra leader should be clipped. They will tolerate less than perfect soil but do not like wet feet. Oriental Spruce is as close as it gets to a maintenance free tree. Plant it, feed it a balanced fertilizer for a few years, stand back and let it go. By 2217 it will be a tourist attraction.

A dark green Oriental Spruce planted in the woods on the upper end of Buffalo Road.

The Cedars

Red Cedar

Cedar is one of those tree names attributed to a lot of trees that are not cedars. Red Cedar, you know the one, an upright evergreen you see all up and down Interstate 77, usually a lot of them together, they are not cedars, they are junipers. That "cedar" siding you see on cabins around the county is not cedar, it is arborvitae. The Alaskan Cedar, a very pretty, tall, weeping evergreen tree, there is one in front of Ashe Memorial Hospital, is a false cypress. Odd that a tree would be named "false" unless it were a tree named

This isn't a Cedar; although almost everyone calls this tree Red Cedar, it is really a Juniper.

Someone long ago planted these two "Red Cedars" in front of a now abandoned old house near Lansing.

"cedar" that is not a cedar. The aromatic "cedar" lumber used to line blanket chests and closets to keep moths away is juniper. Those bagged cedar chips you buy at the pet store for the dog house to keep Old Yeller smelling good are juniper too. Maybe it is because "cedar" is two syllables and comes off the tongue easier, or maybe folks do not care what a real "cedar" is, who started this anyway?

There are two varieties of cedar planted in Ashe County and most people would not recognize them as such. Some would call them a pine but they more closely resemble the shape and look of a spruce or fir. Up close their needles are unique frilly little bundles that poke upward along the stem. Their cones are more barrel shaped than elongated and their limbs spread wider from the trunk and take up more space than a pine, spruce or fir.

Here is what a real Cedar looks like. This Deodara Cedar is growing along Highway 88 in Clifton.

Deodara

    The two cedars are distinguished from one another by their color and form. The Deodara Cedar is green, with dark green needles inside and light green needles outside. They are an attractive focal point type tree even as a young tree. They need to be given lots of room. They grow into the largest spreading evergreen tree in this part of the world. Their branches cantilever at regular intervals and nod toward the ground at the very tip. They are graceful, exotic immigrants who find Ashe County to their liking until the temperature dips below −10°F. As a result there are no big old Deodara Cedars in Ashe County.

Atlantic Cedar

The Atlantic Cedar is the other cedar and even though they are hardier than the Deodar there aren't any big old Atlantic Cedars around either. It may be because they have not been planted in Ashe County for very long. There are some around but not many. Their foliage has a blue green cast with more blue than green. When planting them it is good to know they transplant better at a younger, smaller size, preferably in a container. Field grown, balled and burlapped Atlantic Cedars tend to be shaky in the root ball from losing so many lateral roots in the digging process. If you do purchase a balled and burlapped Atlantic Cedar make sure to stake it or the wind will blow it over. Another important planting tip is to protect them from

Betty Rembert

Atlantic Cedar have a blue cast to their foliage and make a good substitute for a Blue Spruce.

Blue Atlantic Cedar are fast growing trees but should be planted as seedlings because they do not transplant well in larger sizes.

deer. There is something about an Atlantic Cedar that compels deer to scrape their antlers on the trunk so make sure to fence them in. If they survive the transplanting and the deer, they grow fast and are another interesting blue tree to add to the landscape.

False Cypress

A terrible name, "False Cypress," for such a beautiful group of trees. There is nothing false about them. They are all evergreen conifers but they also come in various shades of yellow, green and blue. Most false cypresses are dwarf or semi dwarf shrubs. A few of them grow into medium size trees, under fifty feet tall, and a very few others can get up to a hundred feet tall.

In Ashe County the most common false cypresses are the Cripps Cypress, Hinoki Cypress, Boulevard Cypress and the Alaskan Cedar. There is also the half sibling, the Leyland Cypress. None of them, except the Leyland Cypress, are commonly planted here mainly from the lack of availability but they all do well in the High Country.

Hinoki Cypress

The Hinoki (pronounced high-nokey) Cypress is a dark green columnar evergreen with flat sprays of foliage laid out horizontally to the ground. They are not prickly to touch like a lot of other conifers but instead have soft, loose, thick boughs. Hinoki trees are slow growing, as in twenty feet in thirty years, but can reach heights of forty feet in a hundred years. There is a dwarf variety of the Hinoki Cypress that has the identical foliage of the tree variety, and is used as a shrub but stays under ten feet. It is a good idea to know which one you are planting. Hinoki trees make a nice foil for flowers in an English garden setting.

False Cypress

Hinoki Cypress is one of the prettiest ornamental evergreens that require no pruning to maintain their natural form.

Boulevard and Cripps Cypress

The Boulevard Cypress is a bit of a ragamuffin tree. They have soft blue foliage on their outer branches but show dead brown needles behind the outer foliage. Actually blue and brown are good colors together but a lot of folks are put off by it. It is a matter of taste. "Beauty is in the eye of the beholder." Boulevard Cypress add a rugged wildness to the landscape and birds love them. They are thickly foliated but have gaping holes that birds can fly into at full speed and disappear. Many a sharp shinned hawk has been frustrated chasing its supper into a Boulevard Cypress. Their blue foliage is lightest and brightest in the spring, almost as if they were blooming. Like the Hinoki tree they are slow growing but should be given plenty of room for their eventual size. Boulevards tend to be more upright than spreading and make a good hedge or privacy screen without getting too big.

The Cripps Cypress (center) is a type of Hinoki Cypress only faster growing and bright yellow. The Boulevard Cypress (on the right) is a blue cast evergreen, slower growing, coarser and a great bird habitat.

The Cripps Cypress can best be described as captured sunlight. The more sunlight they get the brighter yellow they are. They are brighter yellow on the south side of the tree than on the north side. Planted in partial shade they turn green or chartreuse at best. Cripps Cypress need full sun to show their stuff. They are beautiful year round but come winter they are uplifting to the spirit in all that gray, brown and white. Everyone should have a Cripps Cypress to look at through a big window. They grow into a large medium-size tree. Sounds like an oxymoron but it is true. They spread wide for their height making them a substantial mass of vegetation. Give them plenty of room, full sun and a bird feeder. Get yourself a picture window, a comfortable chair, a footstool, a cup of coffee sweetened with maple syrup and kick back with a Cripps Cypress.

Alaskan Cedar

The Alaskan Cedar is the tallest grower of the group. They can reach a hundred feet in a favorable setting. They are a relative newcomer to Ashe County so there aren't any big ones around, yet. They are easily the most interesting form of the false cypresses. Their weeping habit almost looks like they are melting. They are a very upright slender tree but will bush out if they are topped or denied a leader. Their color can vary from bluish green to greenish blue and their pendulous shape definitely draws attention and conversation. They are so distinctively different looking than any other tree in Ashe County that giving them their own stage is highly recommended.

Leyland Cypress

The Leyland Cypress is not a true false cypress. They are only half false which makes them a true half false cypress. Some folks call that a hybrid. The Leyland Cypress is a cross between the Alaskan Cedar and a Monterey Cypress. They were first hybridized in England in the late nineteenth century but did not catch on until the mid twentieth century. They grow like a weed. In ideal conditions, not Ashe County, they can put on three to four feet of new growth a year. The Piedmont and Coastal Plain are more to their liking.

Alaskan Cedar (not really a cedar), is one of the most graceful trees for its weeping foliage and eventual large size.

Leyland Cypress make a great windbreak or privacy barrier but are not totally hardy in Ashe County. Below zero temperatures and high winds can burn them.

They do okay in Ashe County depending on where they are planted. Temperatures around 0° and high wind can burn them. Below −10° and high wind can kill them. They do better in places protected from the wind; ridges should be avoided. They make a very tall visual barrier but beware, they can also shade out a large swath of ground. Leylands can be sheared but they are such aggressive growers, they are hard to keep up with. They make an excellent shade tree and can be limbed up to look the part. Like the Atlantic Cedar they do best planted out of containers instead of balled and burlapped and they grow so fast you can watch them grow.

Arborvitae

Arborvitae are the sweet smelling cousins of the cypress family. They look similar in many ways to the cypresses but their fruity aroma gives them away. Just break off the tip of a bough, crush it between your fingers and give it a whiff. If you say "wow, that smells great," it's an Arborvitae.

Arborvitae trees were a favorite ornamental at the turn of the twentieth century.

The eastern Arborvitae is native to parts of the southern Appalachians but not Ashe County. They were a popular ornamental evergreen in the nineteenth century when planting non-native trees in your yard had just started to catch on. There were no nurseries to speak of but an Arborvitae growing wild could be transplanted from Tennessee into Ashe County, no problem. Arborvitaes are long lived and some of those trees planted back then are still going strong at old abandoned house sites around the county.

They are not very tall trees at maturity, up to forty feet but they have a wide conical crown and a thick trunk which belies their short stature. Another more recent introduction of Arborvitae to Ashe County is the emerald green giant. They are a fast growing, hardy, bug resistant Arborvitae mainly used for wind break or privacy barrier. They transplant well big or small, container grown or B&B, and as their name implies they are bright green. There are many other types of Arborvitae planted around the county but most are shrubs. Some grow to be very large shrubs and in time, as in a hundred years, could become trees.

The Firs

Almost everyone has heard of the Frasier Fir, "the perfect Christmas tree," but few know much about the Concolor Fir or the Momi Fir.

Concolor Fir

The Concolor Fir was introduced to Ashe County as a potential Christmas tree but they never caught on. Unlike the Fraser Fir, which is a bug magnet and a root rot conveyer, the Concolor Fir is neither. They make a large attractive tree and are sometimes called White Fir because of their light greenish blue color. They are another one of those trees that need to be given plenty of room to grow. They get as big as Norway Spruce and live a long time as well. Their needles are longer than Fraser Fir which gives the Concolor Fir a coarser look. They are a much better ornamental tree than the Fraser because they are maintenance free. There are nurseries in the area that grow Concolor Fir and are usually available balled and burlapped in larger sizes. They transplant well, especially in the fall, so all that needs to be done is plant, fertilize and watch it grow.

Momi Fir

The Momi Fir are rare in Ashe County. Only conifer connoisseurs know about them. From a distance they look a lot like a Fraser Fir, same color and same growth habit. Up close they are much coarser because their needles are three times longer and thicker than the Fraser. Like the Concolor Fir they do not get root rot and pests leave them alone. Momi Fir root stock have been

Concolor Fir look very similar to a Colorado Blue Spruce, not quite as bright blue but blue enough and it has no pest problems.

Momi Fir is another pest free tree and looks like a Fraser Fir on steroids.

grafted to Fraser Fir scion in an attempt to make Fraser Fir resistant to root rot (it works) but it is more time consuming and expensive to graft instead of growing from seed. Momi Fir are an unusual interesting, beautiful landscape tree. They probably cannot be found in any nurseries in or around Ashe County but they can be found on the Internet.

Fraser Fir

The Fraser Fir do not do well as an ornamental tree unless spraying them regularly with pesticides is something you enjoy doing. Their susceptibility to root rot also makes them problematic as there is no effective treatment for root rot. Another bugaboo to be privy to is to avoid planting fruit trees where Fraser Fir have been grown. Root rot can linger for up to five years. Even if the harvested Fraser Firs show no sign of the infestation, they can still be carriers. Other than that the Fraser Fir is the perfect Christmas tree.

Fraser Fir plantations are widespread around Ashe County; Frasers are the number one Christmas tree variety in the U.S.

Fraser Fir trees are trimmed annually to make their foliage denser and the tree more conical.

Ornamental Flowering Trees

Flowering Cherry

Flowering Cherry is arguably the most popular ornamental tree planted in Ashe County. Eleven months out of the year they hang out in all that Gauguin green, Buster brown, concrete gray and snow white, like a caterpillar's chrysalis only to morph into a splendiferous, flowerful, unleashed explosion of spring's essence. They come in every shade of pink, on shapes that both defy and embrace gravity and, not to be too careful with the truth, flowering cherry trees are as pretty as pretty gets.

For those wanting to argue the point of most popular ornamental tree might want to suggest Purple Leaf Plum, Bloodgood Japanese Maple, Fringe Tree, Redbud, Kousa Dogwood or Rose of Sharon. All are beautiful commonly planted trees in the Ashe County landscape and all are worthy of having their horn tooted.

Purple Leaf Plum

The Purple Leaf Plum is known as much for its purply red leaves as its purply pink flowers of spring. They bloom at about the same time as all the early spring blooming trees but after their flower petals fall their leaves are the show. They need full sun for bright color, shade turns them green. Purple Leaf Plum are sometimes referred to as poor man's Japanese Maple because they have similar color but are much less expensive to buy. They are fast growing, bloom consistently, fragrant, relatively disease and bug resistant but are not long lived like the Japanese Maple.

Ornamental Flowering Trees

Weeping Flowering Cherry are a common residential ornamental that bloom bright white or pink in early spring.

Bloodgood Japanese Maple

The Bloodgood Japanese Maple is the best bet among the Red Leaf maples in the county. They rarely get to twenty feet in height because they are susceptible to those wicked late Ashe County freezes. The Easter freeze of 2007 not only knocked the tops out of all varieties of Japanese Maples, it killed many young trees. Bloodgoods are the hardiest of the Japanese varieties and their spring and fall color are unmatched by any red leaf variety tree. Their blooms are inconspicuous, their whirly gig seeds fly everywhere, they get burned some in the spring but they are an A+ landscape tree.

Bloodgood Japanese Maples are the hardiest and brightest red of the commercially available Japanese Maples.

Fringe Tree

Fringe tree is another tree that is barely a tree but the tree police look the other way. Like the flowering cherry, the fringe tree does not have a lot to say for itself when it is not blooming but when it is blooming, it is one of a kind. Their white flowers are fantastically fragrant. They are so aromatic the neighbors will benefit from their sweet scent wafting by on a gentle breeze. Their drooping tendril flowers bloom profusely over the entire tree, top to bottom. Fringe trees are one of those trees that should be planted in

Fringe Trees are slow growing flowering ornamentals with a sweet aroma like no other tree around.

Fringe tree foliage is large leafed and resembles an Avocado tree's foliage.

multiples, the more the better. They come in male and female, both bloom, but only the females have fruit. The blue fruit resemble olives and attract birds. Fringe trees are a must for a scented garden.

Redbud

Redbud trees come in several varieties but all of them have the familiar sharp pink flowers. They are almost native to Ashe County and some folks would say they are native because there are so many of them planted in the county. The thing to notice is their native habitat is understory woods and they are not growing there in the county. There might be some Redbud trees growing in the woods along the Blue Ridge Parkway in a few spots but the rest have been planted or escaped into the landscape. The Green Leaf Red-

Redbud should be called a Pinky Purple Bud Tree. A great addition to any residential or commercial landscape.

bud is the most common but there is a red leaf variety called "Forest Pansy" that has become a popular choice in Ashe County landscapes. Skyline Telephone Company planted some Forest Pansy Redbud trees in front of their warehouse on Radio Hill to break up the monotony of the side of the building. Good choice. Redbud trees do not get too big and are a good selection to plant close to a building. There is a yellow leaf variety of Redbud too but it is not used much because its yellow color makes it look like something is wrong with it.

Kousa Dogwood

The Kousa Dogwood came into its own in Ashe County after the flowering dogwood blight started killing native dogwoods. The Kousa Dogwood

Kousa Dogwood, or Chinese Dogwood, are similar to Flowering Dogwood but bloom later and have no pest problems.

The seed pods turn brilliant pink red and are edible but an acquired taste.

is an oriental variety of dogwood not attacked by the blight. They have a similar bloom that comes after the flowering dogwood bloom in spring and blooms just as heavily. Their fruit, though, is quite a bit different. Instead of the small, bright red, inedible fruit of the native dogwood, the Kousa Dogwood fruit is large, a half inch across, pink red with pronounced goose bumps and edible. The flavor of the Kousa fruit is an acquired taste. The meat of the fruit is yellow, seedy and has a similar consistency to a persimmon and like the persimmon should be eaten when the fruit is fully ripe and soft. Most folks do not acquire a taste for Kousa fruit but it is attractive hanging on the tree, kind of like cherries. If grown in full sun Kousa Dogwood look more like a large shrub than a tree but they can be limbed up into a tree form.

Rose of Sharon

Rose of Sharon is a poetic name for a beautiful summer blooming, small tree or large shrub. Some folks call them hibiscus or althea but they are all one and the same. This is a tree that plant breeders have been playing with for a long time because of their naturally showy, colorful flowers. They come in various shades of purple, pink, almost red and white. Their flower petals can be single, double or multiple and that is where the plant breeders come in. They are breeding for new and different colors and arrangements of flower petals, but not the form of the tree. Rose of Sharon is the most common summer blooming tree in Ashe County. They are to the mountains what Crepe myrtles are to the Piedmont and Coastal Plain, a colorful, long flowering, heat of the summer tree.

The Flowering Cherry, Purple Leaf Plum, Bloodgood Japanese Maple, Fringe Tree, Redbud, Kousa Dogwood and Rose of Sharon can be readily come by in local nurseries. For the most part they transplant well and thrive throughout the county.

Rose of Sharon is a long blooming summer flowering tree that comes in pink, purple, white and red with single or double petals.

Escaped Trees

Escaped trees are not trees freed from bondage. They are non-native trees that like their new home so much they start reproducing and growing in the wild. Some are welcome, like the Mimosa and others are not, like the Chinese Ailanthus. Both of these trees have "escaped" into Ashe County but neither has become an invasive problem.

Chinese Ailanthus

The Chinese Ailanthus, also known as Tree of Heaven, can be found benignly volunteering around the county but in other parts of the state they are malignantly taking over. In those places it is referred to as the tree of hell. They are a large flowering tree but their blooms are inconspicuous and foul smelling. They seem harmless enough growing alongside the road or in someone's yard but beware, this tree can be trouble.

Mimosa

The Mimosa has a much better reputation. They do not grow into large trees that take over woods. They tend to pop up around disturbed ground, vacant lots, the edge of fields and parking lots. Some folks plant them in their yards. They are low growing delicate trees with brittle branches and almost always grow in groups. Mimosa have pink and white frilly headdress-like flowers and fernlike leaves. Their trunks grow angular to the ground and are inviting for kids to climb. They are short lived trees, twenty years or so, but they reseed themselves and left unattended can grow into a coppice.

Mimosa trees have escaped into the wild landscape after being introduced as an ornamental tree but they are not overwhelmingly invasive.

Big Tooth Aspen

The most astounding and rarest escaped tree in Ashe County is the Bigtooth Aspen. They were introduced to North America from Eastern Europe in the 1770s where they spread like fast food franchises from New England to the Great Lakes to the southern Appalachians but now are in retreat. They need fire to regenerate and fire suppression over the last century has cornered the Bigtooth in small patches looking for a match. At Mount Jefferson State Natural Area there is a handful of them below the last overlook before the summit parking lot. More information about the Bigtooth Aspen can be found at the rangers station at the park's gate.

Paulownia

Paulownia are not commonly found in Ashe County but where they pop up they are unmistakably noticeable. They can have leaves as big as a large pizza and sprout up to fifteen feet in a single growing season. They are not com-

Paulownia are an invasive tree but not quite hardy enough to become a problem here in the wild.

pletely hardy in the county, but some do become trees. More often the above ground part of the tree gets killed back in winter but the roots survive. So the root system keeps growing bigger and bigger with more and more nutrient capacity and come spring, what can only be described as an explosion of growth occurs. They end up looking like some kind of tropical jungle plant with their enormous leaves and tall stalk. They make a very interesting landscape plant that can be treated more like a perennial, a gigantic perennial, than a tree. They are best transplanted by root cuttings or sprouts.

There are a few Paulownia trees growing next to the bridge where Buffalo Road and Elliot Road intersect on Highway 88 West and are best viewed in late summer. There is also a mature Paulownia tree near the bridge that has managed to survive the winter cold and blooms its showy violet flowers before it leafs out in the spring.

Cottonwood and Weeping Willow

Cottonwood, weeping willow and water go together like turtles, frogs and ponds. It is only natural to think of them that way, but they can also stand high and dry as well, like box turtles, toads and boulders.

Weeping willows are so common in Ashe County most folks think they

Weeping Willows along the north fork of the New River give a pastoral, sleepy feel to the landscape.

are native but they are not. They are a beloved ornamental tree. Their curtain of long drooping delicate branches falling to the ground are inviting. Just push them aside and go on in. A breeze floats and sways a weeping willow like the skirt of a hula dancer. They are a romantic tree, the mint julep of trees, an Old South tree. A tree to plant next to a pond and cast a line for a bream. A tree to drift by in a flat bottom boat with your lover. Weeping willows conjure summer, heat, swimming and long days. Hamburgers and beer, horseshoes and lying in the grass. Kingfishers, herons, frogs. Katydids, campfires and canoes.

In winters' freezing rain weeping willows collect crystals, sparkling and clattering in the wind and in spring they are green's graceful first arrival. They are an unwritten ode that everyone knows.

Cottonwood trees, on the other hand, are a ramrod of a tree, tall, straight and thick in time. They are extremely fast growing, putting out five to six feet of new growth annually. They are more desirable as an ornamental

Cottonwood trees are true poplars and often planted but can grow into thickets from heavy seeding around themselves.

Cottonwood leaves have the true Poplar shape that distinguishes them from the more common Tulip Poplar.

tree than a tree grown for lumber. Folks like to plant them down by the river because that is where they are supposed to be. They are not as popular as the weeping willow but cottonwood make a great big tree faster than any other tree around. Cottonwood gets its name from the fluffy white catkins they drop in the spring, not from the color of their wood. Their heartwood is brown and their sapwood is white and is not valued for lumber in Ashe County. They are not readily available from nurseries in this area but can be ordered from tree catalogs. They are an excellent erosion control tree but stay away from a septic tank: their roots will clog the works.

Crimson King Norway Maple

The Crimson King Norway Maple is a favorite non-native shade tree. Their husky dark burgundy color in spring is unique in the Ashe County landscape. This is one of those trees best planted twenty-five years ago. They are slow growing. As spring rolls into summer, Crimson Kings get darker and darker red, turning the blackest red known to still be attractive. Very unique. Come fall don't look, just rake the leaves and look ahead. Even though your Crimson King will be a puny little tree for years to come after you plant it, remember they eventually get huge, so give them plenty of room.

Crimson King Norway Maples have dark red leaves most of the summer but continue to darken as the fall approaches, though they aren't known for their fall color.

Ornamental Birches

River Birch

The ornamental birches are a mixed bag in Ashe County. The river birch does the best of the bunch. Their light orange peeling bark on young trees is attractive but they lose that look with age, becoming darker and coarser. They transplant well, are fast growing and hardy. Their M.O. is usually a clump, three or more trunks, but a single trunk is appealing too. River birch are messy trees, they drop leaves and twigs year round, which should be taken into account when placing them in the landscape. There is a perfectly placed river birch at the Ashe County Public Library. Approaching the library, it is on the left on the corner at the turn into the staff parking lot. That tree is also a good example of how tall and wide they get. As a young tree river birch are often planted too close to buildings. River birch are a reliable, good looking tree, in spite of their messy habits, they just need to be put in the right spot.

European Birch

The other ornamental birches are the white barked ones. The European Birch is the most commonly planted white birch in the county, it is the one with very white bark and the irregular black bark particularly at the bottom of the tree. They are strikingly bright, handsome trees that everyone admires. Unfortunately they have a major problem that is very difficult and expensive to control. They are attacked by a nasty bug called the bronze birch borer. They are an insidious pest that attacks mature trees at the top of the tree first where they are difficult to reach with spraying. Most of the time the problem is identified after the damage is done and the tree is beyond saving. It is best

A River Birch in a perfect spot between the Ashe County Public Library and the West Jefferson Park.

European Birch are susceptible to a boring insect and are not long lived as a result.

European Birch have interesting bark but are not a good choice in the Ashe County landscape.

to avoid planting European White Birch in Ashe County no matter how compellingly attractive they are.

Paper Birch

Paper Birch is another commonly planted tree in the county. They are similarly bright white like the European Birch less the black markings, and succumb to the same affliction as their European cousin. They are very beautiful trees but are best planted in Vermont.

A row of Asian Birch a few years after planting and not showing silvery trunks yet, near the Tennessee line; and see facing page.

Asian Birch

The third white birch variety is the Asian Birch. They are the *only* white birch that is resistant to the bronze birch borer in the county but they are not as bright white as the others. They are more silvery white than bright white. It is a tradeoff, live silvery white tree or dead bright white tree. Easy pick but might be hard to find anywhere close by. For folks wanting to find this tree to plant, its botanical name is *Betula platyphylla* and sources are likely found on the Internet.

The same row of Asian Birch but fifteen or twenty years older and bowed over from winter's snow and ice.

Ornamental Pears

There are many varieties of ornamental pears planted in the county, two of which stand out: Bradford and Aristocrat.

Bradford

The Bradford is the most common and the most problematic. Ashe County really is not ornamental pear country. Late spring freezes burn early blooming trees almost every year and late fall deciduous trees tend to get their fall foliage fried before they get a chance to show their colors. Bradford pears have great fall color in November if it does not freeze before then. They are a good gauge of global warming. If they get to show their fall color it means October freezes did not happen. Bradford pears also have a weak stem structure. They branch from a singular point which makes them susceptible to breaking open under the weight of ice and snow. They are also vulnerable to high wind. They are one of the few trees that benefit from pollarding. Cutting them back makes them shorter and stronger.

The late Dr. J.C. Raulston, for whom the North Carolina State Arboretum is named, once recommended that Bradford pears be avoided in the entire state of North Carolina due to their many problems and short life span. Be forewarned.

Aristocrat

Aristocrat pear has a similar look to the Bradford with one important improvement, they do not branch from a singular point on the trunk. They

A row of Bradford Pears that have not been pollarded: still in good shape but vulnerable to the wind, snow and ice.

branch regularly up and down a central trunk, making them less likely to breaking open in ice, snow and wind. Otherwise they share the same early blooming, late fall color problems the Bradford pears do. Plant something else, like a Chinese Chestnut.

Chinese Chestnut

Granted, ornamental pears and Chinese chestnut have very little in common. Chinese chestnut trees are not planted as ornamental trees, they are planted for their nuts. Almost every farm and many yards have Chinese chestnut trees in Ashe County. It is a cultural phenomenon that has little basis in common sense. Chinese chestnuts are pretty good to eat, especially

Chinese Chestnut flowers just starting to appear in early summer.

Chinese Chestnuts in full bloom are low spreading trees and make loads of nuts in the fall.

roasted, but few brag about how good they are. They can be purchased at the Ashe County Farmers Market and local stores but you never hear anyone say "the chestnuts are incredibly good this year." Maybe it is because they are so common and make nuts by the bushel. Ashe County is not known for its Chinese chestnut production even though they grow in abundance. There should be plantations of Chinese chestnut trees shipping nuts all over the world. Making chestnut butter and beer by the barrel. They are full of oil but nobody is making chestnut oil. We could be running our farm equipment on chestnut oil instead of diesel.

Maybe the hulls are the problem. They have to be handled with a gloved hand. You might pick up one chestnut hull bare handed and take a look at it but you will not pick up two. Chestnut hulls have got to be good for something. It just has not been discovered yet.

Chinese chestnut trees are heavy bloomers but wouldn't you know it, their flowers stink. A blooming chestnut tree is nice to look at from a distance. The entire crown is covered in yellow cream colored tendril flowers and they bloom reliably every summer. Why isn't there chestnut honey?

The Chinese chestnut is an Ashe County riddle: What makes food by the ton and is eaten by the ounce?

Catawba Tree

The Catawba tree is also known as catalpa or bean tree and is planted widely around the county and they have also escaped cultivation and volunteered themselves to make the county more beautiful. The Catawba tree on Jefferson Avenue next to the historic Bantam Chef is the best example of this

This Catawba Tree has anchored the gateway to downtown West Jefferson for decades and was until recently the only tree growing on Jefferson Avenue.

picturesque tree in the county and previously mentioned at the end of Part I as an icon of West Jefferson trees.

Every kid that has ever had a curiosity about smoking might have sampled smoking a Catawba tree bean at one time or another. To be sure, it only requires a few puffs to dismiss the fantasy.

Catawba trees are a member of the legume family of plants, which includes peas, beans and locust trees, and explains the trees' huge inedible, unsmokable bean pods. They are often planted as a shade tree as well as an ornamental tree because they are fast growing and get taller than fifty feet. As an ornamental tree they bloom their white clusters of flowers reliably every year at the start of summer. Catawba trees also branch thick limbs at just the right height for hanging a tire swing. They are messy trees when they drop their flowers and beans but they are well worth cleaning up after.

Catawba trees should be available for purchase at local nurseries but, if not, they are easily transplanted from volunteer sprouts in the fall.

Silver Maple

Silver maples are another non-native tree that are so common most folks think they are native. Their natural range covers a wide swath of the eastern half of the continental United States but not the higher elevations of the Appalachian mountains. They can be planted successfully at higher elevations than their natural range but they stay where they are planted and do not spread or escape into the wild.

A giant old Silver Maple just off the four lane between the towns on McConnell Street; the author lends perspective.

Silver Maple leaves have deep cut lobes that give them a Japanese Maple appearance.

Silver maples are very fast growing shade trees that get really big really fast. They can grow a trunk of two to three feet in diameter in just twenty-five years. They grow faster in moist conditions but also do well high and dry.

Silver maple gets its name from the silver color of the underside of its leaves. The top side of the leaves are light green but when the wind blows, the silver underside turns up and flashes silver. Their leaves are deeply notched and resemble the cut leaf of some Japanese maples. They are attractive trees with their flashy leaves and silvery bark, but they are also messy, twiggy trees that drop detritus year round. Ice, snow and wind contribute to their untidiness. Like the Bradford Pear, the silver maple takes pollarding and pruning well, which keeps them from breaking apart in storms. In addition to their fast growing massive trunks, they have massive root systems. Planting them near buildings, walls, sidewalks and septic systems should be avoided. They like water and can be used to help dry up a wet place in a yard which also makes them grow faster.

Silver maples can be tapped for making maple syrup but it takes a lot more sap to make half as much syrup. In some circles silver maple is known as a "poor man's maple" for its low sugar count but he would have to have a rich man's firewood shed to boil all the sap needed to make syrup. Silver maple syrup has good flavor and is worth its weight in gold.

Though silver maple syrup is a rare, delicious treat the tree's best attribute is its fast growing nature. During the course of a lifetime, sixty to seventy years, a silver maple can grow to six feet in diameter and seventy-five feet tall. Make sure to get your parents to plant one when you are born, they are readily available at nurseries and in tree catalogs.

Part IV: Tree Culture

Tree Nursery

Trees have been cultivated for ornamentation, timber, fruit, nuts and foliage for thousands of years. They idea of growing trees in a more convenient, controlled setting probably went hand in glove with domesticating plants of all kinds, whether for food, medicine, material, or beauty. Trees just take longer. Patience is a required prerequisite for tree growers.

Growing Fraser Fir into Christmas trees is a good example of the test of

A field-grown ornamental tree nursery in the Clifton Community below Jonasee Rock during winter.

Balled and burlapped ("B&B") ornamental evergreens ready to be planted into a new landscape.

time. First the Fraser Fir seeds are sown in a bed of loose chemically sterilized soil with regulated fertilization and irrigation. The resulting seedlings stay in the same bed for three years before they are dug up bare root and replanted in a new bed further apart. Then they spend another two years growing to a height of twelve to fifteen inches, at which point they are again dug up bare root and planted out in a field. It then takes about another seven or eight years before they are ready to harvest. That is a twelve or thirteen year timetable and commitment to grow a tree ready for market. In comparison, pumpkins take about four or five months to bring to market…

Growing white pines for timber takes three times longer than growing Fraser Fir for Christmas trees. It takes thirty to forty years to grow white pine into saw timber. The process also begins in a nursery where seeds are sown in a bed to be grown into transplants that are big enough to be planted in the field.

Newly planted Fraser Fir seedlings in irrigated beds where they will grow for a couple of years into transplants.

Usually white pine transplants are set out on a site where hardwoods have been harvested by clear cutting. The white pines grow faster than hardwood trees which require about fifty or sixty years to become saw timber. Sometimes pastureland is retired into growing white pine for timber. Trees do not have to be fenced like cattle, they tend to stay where they are planted.

Logging is an important agricultural enterprise in Ashe County. Almost every farm has timber acreage that gets handed down through the generations or gets bought and sold. Whether logging native hardwoods from nat-

Logged over land being grazed by a herd of goats with no cover crops sown to prevent erosion.

ural stands or planted boundaries, farmers usually sell their timber to logging companies instead of cutting it themselves. The logger has the specialized equipment and machines to harvest the timber and offers the farmer a price or buys it on shares, splitting the proceeds as agreed upon.

Most logged over land is not replanted with nursery grown seedlings but instead is left to regrow from natural seeding and regrowth from stumps. Remarkably, a forest will regrow itself in Ashe County if the land is left alone. Nutrient rich soil, abundant rainfall, tree varieties with winged seeds and birds all contribute to regenerating native trees into a forest.

Ornamental tree nurseries are not as plenteous as Christmas tree farms or timber boundaries but they do get invited to the ball. They can be Cinderella during an economic boom but the coach always turns into a pumpkin when there is a bust. Ornamental tree nurseries are dependent on new construction for their success, which comes to a screeching halt with every recession. During the "Great Recession" of the late 2000s more than half of the ornamental tree nurseries in the county went out of business and the ones that survived were the ones that also grew Christmas trees.

The farmers that grow ornamental trees exclusively are called nurserymen or nurserywomen. They are also called dreamers and artists. They see the landscape like a blank canvas in need of some paint and a brush. Ornamental trees are three dimensional yard art. They gift terra firma with the luxury of eye candy. Ornamental trees are not needed, they are wanted.

Ornamental tree growers are like river boat gamblers floating a river through a desert. When they play blackjack they say "hit me" when they are showing two kings. They take cuttings from trees growing in cemeteries. They will grow a tree nobody has ever heard of just to educate the public. They are optimists of renown.

Growing ornamental trees is not as slow as growing Christmas trees but unlike Christmas trees, ornamental trees are not valuable dead. They have

Landscape gardening is like painting a picture in three dimensions that continuously changes from daylight to dark, from season to season.

to be sold alive with a root ball attached at the bottom. A shovel or a tree spade instead of a chain saw is required at harvest. Getting to the harvest can be tedious but typically ornamental trees grow more vigorously in their first five years than Fraser Fir. Some trees will be ready to sell in five years or less depending on how they are marketed. Some trees are sold as "whips" which describes their limbless trunk. A whip can be grown from a cutting (clone), seed or graft and is only a year or two old when it can be transplanted bare root or from a container. This size tree is most often grown out to a larger size in another nursery setting, either in containers or in nursery beds, then transplanted again. But not necessarily. A whip is typically one to three feet tall and can be planted directly in the field or landscape if desired.

Some tree nurseries grow nothing but seedlings, whips or grafts for resale to field grown nurseries. The trees are started or propagated in unheated greenhouses in containers, flats or beds to protect them from early or late freezes depending on the season, to control watering and fertilization and to extend the growing season. Other nurseries grow their own nursery stock to transplant to a field grown setting and still others do both, growing their own and buying transplants in.

Growing trees from seeds is more often than not the easiest, least expensive way to grow a tree. Some tree varieties will germinate and take root in a natural outdoor setting, just like planting a vegetable garden in the spring. Some varieties need coaxing in the nursery or greenhouse to enhance germination, such as artificially exposing them to controlled cold temperatures in a refrigerator for a set period of time to get the seeds to germinate. Others need to be dried out and still others need to be soaked, or both, to stimulate germination. Each and every tree variety has its own schedule and needs and the nursery has to know every nuance of every variety they grow to be successful.

Growing trees from cuttings is another technique for propagation that can be amazingly easy or disturbingly frustrating. Most cuttings can be taken in spring before new growth begins or some must be taken from the new growth. Some varieties of trees can be forced to root in a cold frame with heated beds or flats during the late fall and winter. Cuttings taken in the late fall need to have been exposed to a hard freeze before they are cut. Not all tree varieties necessarily root well so those that do not root well but root enough to make it worthwhile must be cut in greater quantities to ensure the volume needed. Other tree varieties might root 100 percent and fewer cuttings are needed.

Grafting takes the most time and skill to propagate trees but is still a low tech hands-on method. All it requires is a very sharp knife and steady hands. Of course there are specialized tools and materials that make it go faster and easier but if you are just grafting a few trees or buds what is needed can be found around the house. A sharp knife, a rubber band and a little candle wax.

There are a number of techniques to graft trees, none of which will be addressed here. Too long of a subject. Whole books have been written about grafting. Check them out or go online. The bottom line is it takes two trees to make one. One has to have a root system, the other does not and they are joined as one. Grafting is usually done to ensure variety, vigor, gender and size. Once a graft has taken hold and joined together the tree grows into what was attached to the part that has roots. Most often root stock is produced from seeds grown from like varieties in seedling beds until it is big enough to host the desired variety grafted to it, called scion or "sign wood." Sometimes the root stock will send out a shoot and compete with the scion and must be removed. A shoot growing off the root stock is sometimes called a "sucker" because they tend to grow more vigorously than the grafted scion and rob the graft of nutrients which can stunt its growth. If the sucker is not removed soon enough it can overpower the desired graft to a point the graft is no longer viable and the tree has to be destroyed.

Suckers are also called graft jumpers and it is a problem that can occur indefinitely. As a grafted tree matures, graft jumpers sprouting from the root system tend to disappear but not necessarily. If a sucker appears even one time on a grafted tree, it is a good idea to be vigilant in the future and look for it to happen again. A pair of clippers will solve the problem for now but keep an eye out in the years to come.

There are other ways to propagate trees than mentioned here, like a technique called tissue culture, but which require specialized equipment. Other grafting techniques get a bit too technical to explore here and become "the science of growing trees," so you will have to look elsewhere to dig deeper in those realms.

Four Seasons

In Ashe County the seasons line up almost exactly like they do on the calendar. Starting with the vernal equinox, take a look up at the side of a tree covered mountain and notice the light red hue in the top of the trees, the blush is the first sign the trees are waking up, winter is over, the saps a-rising. If there is a weeping willow around, they have already greened up, buckeye

A Cherry Tree along a farm road in full bloom in spring and the grass greening up from winter.

Summer in Ashe County off the beaten path, a craggy old Sugar Maple above it all. And see front cover.

buds are swollen and red, aiming to be the first trees to leaf out. On the forest floor in the last week of March trout lilies, hepatica and cut leaf toothwort seem to come out of nowhere with blooms. Migratory birds are on the move. Tree swallows have arrived from South America. Robin flocks leapfrog through the woods in no apparent hurry but relentlessly on the move. Bluebirds' blue backs catch the eye, a welcome color anytime but especially in spring. Doves are cooing. Frogs are peeping and croaking, laying their eggs in ponds and low lying pools. Spring brings rain and wet snow, sometimes heavy, uprooting trees and knocking down limbs, mother nature's way of culling and pruning the forest. The red maples are in full bloom by April Fool's Day and serviceberry is not far behind. The birds unite to sing their cacophony chorus at dawn, bringing in the day with their chatter, gossip and excitement. Spring in the woods is an amorphous rush to unleash procreation in all its fecund forms. Fertility flows out of the cold and ice of winter like a warm wind throbbing with new life.

Ashe County is reliably rainy in spring and notorious for late snows and freezes. In the spring of 2000 there were three straight nights of hard freezes the last week of May. The aftermath looked like there had been a fire in the New River valleys. It was a very strange sight exaggerated by the fact there was no damage to the trees above 3300 feet of elevation. It gave the appearance the valley had been flooded and after the water receded had left a bathtub ring. The freezes occurred the way they did because there had been no wind to stir the atmosphere and the heavy cold air settled in the valleys. Temperatures on the valley floor were ten to fifteen degrees colder than the tops of the surrounding ridges. The temperature above 3300 feet had remained above freezing while the valley froze. The damage was extensive. New growth

The south fork of the New River meanders through a fall landscape that's picture perfect.

Winter and a hungry crow eyes the frozen apples still clinging to the tree.

on Christmas trees was killed back to the old growth. Gardens, even those that had been covered, were killed back to the ground. Folks called it a freak freeze that only happens every one hundred years or so. No one had ever seen anything like it.

On April 5, 2007, Easter Sunday, a winter storm hit Ashe County after weeks of unseasonably warm weather in March. The storm dumped four inches of powdery crystalline snow, the temperature dropped to 15°F with a forty-five mile an hour wind. The storm was so extreme that local nurseries lost a high percentage of their plants and those that survived had the tops knocked out of them. It was a devastating year to be in the nursery business but it did not damage the Christmas trees or any conifers. Folks had never seen anything like it, it was a freak storm that only happens every hundred years or so. There were no cherries, apples, peaches, plums or blueberries that year. If you are counting, that is two 100-year freezes seven years apart.

Spring and the trees and grass are waking up from their winter sleep.

By mid–May the stunning transformation from gray mountains to green mountains has reset the color code from our eyes to our brains. The change happens over a period of weeks but once it is green again it seems like it happened overnight. The landscape has totally filled with greenery so lush and rich it is hard to think it was ever anything else. By the summer solstice the herbaceous undergrowth in the woods is so thick, it is not a walk in the woods anymore, it is a wade in the woods. Stinging nettle is waist deep and a walking stick or gloved hands are required to push it aside. You cannot see your shoes. There could be an innocent snake lying there that scares you both to death when you discover each other. Spiders have webbed the woods in a way that everything from the ground to ten feet up is a trap. Gnats flit annoyingly all around your face and occasionally fly in your eyes, up your nose, in your ears or you swallow one while you are yawning. The lush patches of stinging nettle can abruptly change into a sea of white snake root and then to poison ivy in a heartbeat—which accelerates when you realize you are surrounded by poison ivy.

Yellow jackets and hornets build nests in trees and in the ground. The rare copperhead or rattlesnake can freeze you in your tracks. More often it is a black rat snake, a milk snake or a garter snake checking you out. They blend into the landscape so perfectly they are seldom seen.

Pileated woodpeckers jackhammer rectangular holes in dead and dying trees, flying from one tree to the next blaring their Appalachian Tarzan call. Multitudes of exotic migratory birds return to the woods of spring and summer with their songs, tropical fish colors and nesting instincts. Salamanders, centipedes, millipedes, ants, beetles, ring-neck snakes and worms are under nearly every rock and rotting log. Bee balm, bergamot, horse balm. Fox grape and Indian pipe vine. Greenbriar and blackberries. Golden Alexander, columbine and meadow rue. Deciduous hollies and goosefoot maples. Chicken of the woods, chanterelles, morels and death angels. Moss, lichens

A bright green meadow in the bottom land along the south fork of the New River.

and liverworts. More than seven hundred species of plants and fungi live in and on the woods of Ashe County. Watch where you are stepping.

Ashe County is a humid place in summer but not too hot. Some folks complain when the temperature hovers around 90°F but it is always cool in the shade and there is lots of shade. The mixed hardwood forest forms a high dense canopy over the forest floor where it usually stays moist and cool but during persistent drought conditions can become dry and tinder. Forest fires are rare during summer when the forest floor is covered in thick herbaceous greenery and thunder storms randomly roll through dumping rain so hard and fast most of it runs off but elevates the humidity.

Summer is the time trees grow. If there is plenty of rain trees can add a couple of feet of new growth but if the weather is dry they will not grow much at all. Looking at tree rings of an older tree on a fresh cut stump can show the wet years from the dry ones. The rings will be wider and further apart during a wet growing season and closer together during years of drought. Trees are survivors. During times of drought they hang on not growing much but during years of ample rain their growth rate takes off. Trees are adaptable. Like us they have no say about where they arrive in this world. A seed can land in a crevice in a rock and germinate in less than desirable conditions. If the seed came from a mighty oak it has the potential to be that too, but if there is not enough soil and moisture in the crevice the seedling will not have the opportunity to fulfill its potential. It is capable though of adapting to its predicament. It can grow very, very slowly and survive for many, many years. Trees are resourceful.

As summer moves along, tree growth slows down and as the days grow shorter the leaves start to shut down their manufacturing of nutrients from sunlight, at which point they begin to die and change colors. It is one of the great wonders of the world to watch deciduous trees change from the green of summer to the warm colors of the light spectrum during the fall. Buckeye trees are the first trees to leaf out in the spring and the first to lose their leaves in late summer. They are the semaphore of spring and the harbinger of fall. When folks think of fall in Ashe County they are really thinking about the month of October when the leaves change color and then fall off the trees. The last week of September usually still feels and looks like summer. In November the clock gets set back, it gets dark in the afternoon and 8 p.m. feels like midnight. The trees look like they all died and the woodshed is full and

Fall Maples in all their red and orange glory light up the landscape as if plugged into electricity.

stacked to the roof. December can be just as wintery as January but with the warming climate winter is not what it used to be.

Fall is all about the trees. Tourists flock to Ashe County like migratory birds to see the show of color from the trees. Every rental cabin, motel room, restaurant and parking place is full. The streets of West Jefferson are packed with pedestrians looking for something to buy, or maybe they are just looking. The colorful forests of Mount Jefferson and Paddy Mountain loom above town with their spectacular display of warm, cozy orange, red and yellow. On a crystal clear Carolina blue sky fall day, it is a great day to be in Ashe County. The colors do not last long enough though. The peak of colors lasts less than a week and some folks say it only lasts for a day. "Today is the peak" and you know it when you see it. It is as ephemeral as a morning glory flower, temporal as tomorrow and as elusive as yesterday. The next thing you know it is snowing, the wind is howling and you are putting studded tires on your Subaru. The days keep getting shorter and trucks hauling Christmas trees fill the highways. Another wave of tourists come to cut their own Christmas tree at local farms and then it is Thanksgiving. The Fraser Fir goes up in the den with all the trimmings and there is turkey, taters, hanovers, green bean casserole, cranberry sauce, gravy, pumpkin pie and all the fixings. It is opening day of rifle season for deer and the hunters hit the woods.

Protected Land

Three Top Mountain, between Warrensville and Creston, and Pond Mountain, on the Tennessee, Virginia line, have thousands of acres of state game land for hunting. Three Top is a rugged, steep, heavily forested tract of land and is not for the out of shape, couch potato weekend warrior. The summit of Three Top is the highest elevation 360° view in the county and from there you are overlooking the tens of millions of trees that call Ashe County home. All terrain vehicles are banned on Three Top but obnoxious trespassers ignore the law and drive up there anyway. Too lazy to walk. There is only one game warden monitoring the state game lands and the ATV hucksters take advantage. The same thoughtless yahoos tear up the trail with their spinning tires and do nothing to maintain the trail. Three Top Mountain is one of the most beautiful natural areas in Ashe County but is best avoided during hunting season. Off season is a hiker's delight. There are high elevation stunted forests of beech, oak, maple, Mountain Ash and birch along with a wonderland of rhododendron, Mountain Laurel and blueberries. Rumor has it that the state wildlife folks released rattlesnakes up there too and now they are thicker than flies on a cow pie, but do not believe everything you think. The forests that cover Three Top Mountain are a nature lover's dream.

Pond Mountain, unlike Three Top, is almost totally bald with some of the best views anywhere. There are patches of trees here and there but it is mostly wide open terrain. The Summit is another high elevation 360° view but the view is marred by an ugly Quonset airplane hangar. Before being a game land preserve, Pond Mountain had been a huge Christmas tree farm with a gravel road along its ridge and many side roads to access the Christmas trees. Trucks and ATVs are allowed on the preserve which makes it much easier to get around. It is the perfect hunting preserve for hunters who do

Three Top Mountain really has seven tops and stretches from Warrensville to Creston.

not like to walk. It appears as though the state has no intention of maintaining the Bald and will allow it to return to forest. Check back in a hundred years.

Ashe County is fortunate to have as much protected land and forest as it does. Mount Jefferson State Natural Area, Three Top game land, the Peak, the two New River State Parks, Paddy Mountain, the Nature Conservancy's Bluff Mountain Nature Preserve, Pond Mountain game land, and Phoenix Mountain and the Blue Ridge Parkway all have different levels of protection and public access.

The Bluff Mountain Nature Preserve is accessed by permission or guided tours only. This preserve has some of the rarest ecologies and biodiversity in the southern Appalachian mountains and tours can be arranged through the Nature Conservancy website.

Phoenix Mountain has partial protection of its ridge and is owned by the Nature Conservancy as well. As of the fall of 2017, it is closed to public access.

The Peak, like its neighbor Three Top Mountain, is a steep, rugged, wooded preserve but currently has no public access or trails. A plan for a trail is in the works.

West Jefferson is located at the foot of Paddy Mountain. Most of the protected land on Paddy Mountain is on the ridge and it is owned by the state. There are no current plans for public access at this time. It is also a very steep, rugged, wooded mountain that is best served to be left alone and wild. It is a good idea to let some places be. It is doing fine on its own.

Mount Jefferson State Natural Area (formerly State Park) offers a paved road to near the summit, with overlooks, hiking trails, picnic tables and shelters open to the public during daylight hours.

The Blue Ridge Parkway is federally protected and maintained. It follows the eastern continental divide along Ashe County's eastern boundary and is open year round except during inclement weather. The Blue Ridge Parkway is a magnificent example of what a road can be. No billboards. No trash. No traffic lights. Beautiful scenery and millions of trees.

Winter in Ashe County is similar to southern New England. Snowy, windy and cold enough to cause a lot of folks to flee to warmer places. Winter is a time to hunker down by the fire and rest a bit. Listen to the wind buffeting the house and roaring through the trees. There is a lot less traffic and plenty of parking in West Jefferson near where you are going. There are truckloads of firewood for sale parked alongside the road. Trucks with snow plows and salt spreaders are prowling the back roads. Dead Christmas trees and road kill deer share the shoulders of the road. Hunting season is over and the woods are quiet except for the wind.

Winter is a great time to get out and walk in the woods. The annual summer vegetation has all died off and the woods are open. There are views off through the trees that are not there any other time of year. Ancient boulders dressed with lichens and mosses are mother nature's sculpture garden. You can see where you are going and where you have been. There are no snakes or spider webs. Footing can be slippery especially if there is ice and snow but there is no hurry. The trunks of trees are like columns holding up the sky. Winter in the woods can be awe inspiring. The woods are calling, "Come on in."

LISA CAMP

The most beautiful road anywhere is the Blue Ridge Parkway built along the Continental Divide where it eases along the eastern edge of Ashe County.

Maple Syrup

Historically there is no record of maple syrup being produced commercially in Ashe County. Nonetheless, maple syrup and maple sugar have been made by individuals for their own use for centuries. Almost every old farmhouse in the county has sugar maple trees planted around it. Sugar maple trees make beautiful shade trees but the number one reason they were planted was for their sugar. They were the only source of sugar available for the first European settlers. Honeybees were introduced later.

Legend has it that Native Americans taught the settlers about maple syrup. Supposedly the Native Americans made maple syrup by heating rocks and putting the red hot rocks into a wooden trough filled with sap. The process had to be repeated over and over again to finally get to the sugar. A slow, laborious way to go, but ultimately an effective way to boil off the water in the sap. Unlike many natives, settlers had iron kettles to hang over a fire to boil off the sap, which sped the process considerably.

Since those primitive days of boiling sap down to syrup, new technology has sped up the process dramatically. The latest state of the art uses reverse osmosis to remove some of the water from the sap before it is evaporated, greatly reducing the amount of time to boil off the sap. Instead of a kettle over an open fire, the heat is drawn through flues at the bottom of a pan that increase the surface area in contact with the heat by ten times. And the steam coming off the flue pan is captured by another pan called a steam away which preheats and distills water from the sap before it enters the flue pan, nearly doubling reduction, cutting fuel considerably.

Most commercial maple syrup producers no longer use buckets to collect sap but instead pipe the sap coming out of the trees to a central reservoir. In addition to piping the sap some producers also apply vacuum to the pipes

The Sugar House at Waterfall Farm going full blast evaporating maple sap in February.

to suck the sap from the trees, none of which injures the tree. Maple syrup production has come a long way since boiling with hot rocks.

Winter is maple syrup season in Ashe County. From mid–January to mid–March sap can be collected from native sugar maples and red maples to boil down into syrup. It sounds easy enough but there is a catch: 98 percent of the sap is water and less than 2 percent is sugar. The process of making maple syrup is entirely evaporative: 98 percent of the sap goes up in steam.

Wheeler Munroe just starting up the wood fired evaporator for a day of boiling sap and bottling syrup (inside the building on the facing page).

It takes a lot of fuel and a lot of time. It can take anywhere from fifty to seventy gallons of sap to make a gallon of syrup depending on the amount of sugar in the sap.

Most folks do not measure the amount of sugar in the sap, it is too discouraging, and it takes a hydrometer or a refractometer to measure it. Syrup makers know the sugar is in there but it is going to take a while to get to it.

The first step in making maple syrup is identifying the trees to be tapped. Make sure the trees are maples. The tree should be a minimum of seven inches in diameter four feet off the ground. Any tree from seven inches to fifteen inches in diameter is a one tap tree. Any tree bigger than fifteen inches is a two tap tree and there is no such thing as a three tap tree. Some folks put more than two taps on big old trees but it is not recommended for the long term health of the tree.

Sugar maple trees are supposed to have the highest sugar content compared to other kinds of maples but that is not necessarily true. They probably average higher sugar content than other maples but each and every tree can have different concentrations of sugar. Red maples, silver maples, Norway maples and Ash Leaf maples all have sugar in their sap and can be tapped as well, but it will probably take more sap from them than it would from sugar maples to make syrup. The flavor of the syrup can vary from one type of maple to another and mixing the sap of different kinds of maples can influence the flavor too. Early season syrup tends to be lighter in color and every run of syrup from one day to the next can be a different color and flavor. Often there will be notes of flavor in the syrup like marshmallow, vanilla, butterscotch, caramel, cotton candy, candied apples and cherries.

Maple sap flows are triggered by freeze and thaw cycles. After a freeze, during a thaw, is when the sap is collected. It will run for a few days during a thaw but if it does not freeze again soon the flow will stop. Cold nights and warm days above freezing get the sap flowing. There are many variables at play that make for a strong or weak flow. Barometric pressure influences a run. Sap runs stronger during low barometric pressure than high pressure. Maple trees have measurable pressure inside them that move the sap up and down the trunk. If the barometric pressure is higher on the outside of the tree than on the inside, the tree cannot release the sap. Rain, snow and ice factor in sap flow. Sap flows better during wet weather than dry weather.

To get the sap out of a maple tree an inch and a half deep hole is bored into the tree about four feet off the ground using a drill or a brace and bit. The hole should be drilled at a right angle to the trunk. A hole drilled at a downward angle will be oblong or out of round and cause the tap to leak. After removing the drill bit from the hole, the hole must be cleaned out with a piece of wire or a dry, clean stick. Do not blow in the hole, avoid contaminating the hole with bacteria from your breath or cleaning tool. Bacteria causes the hole to seal itself off and reduce or stop flow of the sap. A spout is then hammered gently but firmly into the hole and a bucket hung underneath.

Spouts can be homemade from a number of different materials. Staghorn Sumac branches make good spouts. The wood inside of the branch is pithy and easily bored out and made hollow. Cut a length about four inches long, remove the bark and shave one end to fit the hole bored in the tree. Do not use green wood. It can contaminate the hole and will shrink and leak as the

Taps hand carved from native Elderberry bushes work just fine for tapping the trees and steering the sap into buckets.

wood dries. Make the Staghorn Sumac or Elderberry spouts ahead of time so they are good and dry.

Wooden dowels can be bored out and made into spouts, and metal flashing can be rolled into the right shape and size too. Whatever material is used, whether store bought or homemade, it should be sterile and dry before being inserted into the tree. Before the next season begins, used spouts should be boiled and dried to ensure they are bacteria free.

Elderberries are juicy and can be made into jams and wine as well as eaten raw.

Spouts that are commercially produced come in three diameters: seven-sixteenths of an inch, five-sixteenths and three-sixteenths. They are made of metal or plastic and some have a hook on them to hang a bucket or plastic bag. There have been a wide variety of spout designs over the last couple of hundred years but most commercially available spouts for hanging a bucket or a bag are similar and straightforward to use.

The spout conveys the sap out over the bucket where it drips and collects. Make sure to use food grade buckets whether they are metal or plastic. A two gallon capacity bucket is ideal but sometimes has to be emptied more than once a day over the course of a strong sap flow. It is a good idea to have empty buckets at sunset because a flow can continue into the night if it stays warm. Having some kind of lid on the bucket that allows sap flow but keeps out rain or snow is a good idea too. Sometimes temperatures will drop and freeze the sap in the bucket. If the ice is floating on top of the sap some folks throw it away because it has less sugar in it and the sap underneath is more concentrated.

Harry Beard sitting by his backyard makeshift evaporator keeping the fire stoked and the sap boiling near the Lihue Knob.

Maple sap should be clear as water coming from the tree but can become cloudy towards the end of the season. At that point the season is coming to an end. The sap is excellent to drink straight from the bucket when it is fresh and cold. It is like drinking spring water with a hint of sweetness. As the sap turns cloudy, though, it loses its sweetness and starts tasting like a paper spit ball and it is time to call it a season.

Next comes the boiling and evaporation. To maximize evaporation a strong boil should be maintained at all times. Losing the boil slows the process. It is best to have a pan or pot with a wide bottom. The wider the surface area exposed to the heat the quicker the evaporation. It is also a good idea to have two pans of sap on the heat, one for hard boiling and the other to preheat the sap. Adding cold sap to a hard boil douses the boil but adding preheated sap helps keep the boil going.

People who heat with wood can use the wood stove to evaporate sap and humidify the house at the same time. It takes a lot longer this way but it works. Sap can spoil. Think of it as tree juice. It needs to be kept cold while waiting to be boiled off. Just keep adding sap to the pot on the stove until it runs out. When it has cooked down to nearly syrup, take it off the wood stove and finish it on a cook stove.

A candy thermometer or hydrometer is needed to get the concentration of sugar just right. When using a candy thermometer the syrup is ready when the temperature reaches 7°F above the temperature at which water boils. Since water boils at different temperatures according to elevation above sea level and present barometric pressure, the thermometer needs to be calibrated for current readings to be accurate. To do this, bring a pot of water to a boil and measure the temperature of the water while it is boiling. If it is boiling at say 209°F the syrup will be ready when it reaches a temperature of 216°F. If the temperature goes higher than 216°F the syrup will be thicker when it cools and may even crystalize some. Also beware of burning or scalding the syrup once the 7°F threshold has been exceeded. Maple sugar candy can be made by continuing the evaporative process but it must be done on a lower heat source or in a double boiler.

If the syrup is going to be bottled for long term storage the temperature of the syrup should be above 180°F when poured into the bottles. To ensure a good seal the bottles should be turned on their sides or turned upside down for a few minutes to heat the lids.

There are quite a few backyard sugarers in Ashe County but only one commercial producer of maple syrup. Waterfall Farm is the only North Carolina Department of Agriculture inspected maple syrup producer in the state of North Carolina. They are licensed to sell their syrup directly to the public at the farm or at the Ashe County Farmers Market. They are not licensed to sell syrup for resale or wholesale. Waterfall Farm is located near Warrensville in the Clifton Community. The farm annually participates in the Blue Ridge Women in Agriculture Farm Tour and welcomes guests to the farm by appointment, especially during the sugaring season.

Ashe County maple syrup is like no other syrup anywhere. The soil, rain, snow, sun and latitude all come together to give its syrup a unique flavor, unsurpassed wherever maple trees are tapped.

Apples

Of all the trees introduced to Ashe County, apple trees are the most legendary, enigmatic, problematic, romanticized and beloved. Apple history probably coincides with the first European settlers in the county, as mentioned earlier. Apples were the number one cultivated source of alcoholic beverages, mainly hard cider, for those early pioneers. But apples were also an important and versatile part of their diet. Apples are rich in vitamins and minerals, though early settlers knew little about nutrition. Apples were a food that could be stored to eat later. They could be buried in the ground whole, packed in straw or leaves to dig up as needed. They could be stored in a root cellar or a spring house and slices of apples could be strung up or laid out to dry. Dried apples, sometimes called apple leather, concentrated the sugar and made for a tasty treat. Some apple trees would not drop their fruit in the fall. The apples would cling to the stem well into winter and be picked and eaten frozen directly from the tree. Apple trees would also attract wildlife like deer, bear, opossum, raccoon, squirrel, turkey and grouse that made hunting and trapping for meat much easier. Cooking the meat, apples were used to flavor and sweeten. Planted apple tree orchards would birth wild apple trees through the digestive tracts of wildlife, then be discovered in the wild and brought back to the farm to be propagated. Apples gave food, flavor, sweets and intoxication to what was otherwise a very difficult way of life.

Growing apples for home use is an Ashe County tradition. Every farm has at least a few apple trees whether they were planted or not. There are some orchards in the county that sell apples but not many. Ashe County is not commercial apple growing country. As of 2017 Big Horse Creek Farm is the only full time apple farm in the county. They sell apples from their two hundred and fifty tree orchard at the Ashe County Farmers Market in down-

An old apple tree left unpruned for years out in a meadow in full bloom making apples for wildlife.

town West Jefferson and to Molley Chomper's Cidery in Lansing, but they butter their bread selling the dream of apples. They sell grafted apple trees in two gallon buckets ready to plant in the field. Every year they graft 3,500 apple trees and 350 varieties. Big Horse Creek Farm, owned and operated by Ron and Suzanne Joyner, specialize in heirloom apples and are committed to keeping the story of heirloom apples alive. No easy undertaking. Bear, deer and rabbits think the Joyners planted the apple trees for them. And there is the predictably unpredictable weather. Late spring freezes when the trees are blooming, sub-zero weather in winter, drought, bugs and fungi. In spite of that, they have succeeded in rejuvenating many heirloom varieties that would have otherwise been lost. They have also introduced two new varieties to the world that were found growing wild on their own land. One is a large red apple they named "Husk Sweet." (Husk is the name of their community.) Ron describes it as a "good kids apple" because they are sweet and crisp but he lets bad kids eat them too. The other apple they named "Husk spice" because it is tart instead of sweet but also has a pleasant crispness that snaps off in your mouth.

Molley Chomper Cidery is an up and coming orchard in Sturgill with about 900 young apple trees. Currently they buy in most of the apples for making their hard cider but intend to eventually have enough of their own apples to supply their cidery.

Historically there have been commercial family owned apple orchards in Ashe County but they have never been large scale. Most orchards were grown for supplemental and seasonal income. A good example was John Little's orchard that used to be along the north fork of the New River at the mouth of Copeland Road on Highway 88 West. John worked at the old Thomasville Furniture Plant in downtown West Jefferson, grew burley tobacco and raised beef cattle. His orchard drew a crowd every fall when he sold apples out of his garage and apple cellar. His orchard was a landmark in the Clifton community during the latter part of the twentieth century.

Another well known orchard in the county was Swansie Shepherd's Orchard and Blueberry Farm. Like John Little, Swansie had a full time job as school teacher and farmed apples, blueberries and sheep on the side. He designed and built his own hydraulic apple press and sold fresh pressed apple juice for a dollar a gallon. If you brought your own apples he would press them for the same price. For weed control he grazed sheep in the orchard and sold the fleece from the sheep annually. Swansie Shepherd was a resourceful man. He kept bees on the second floor porch of his house to pollinate his apples and blueberries and sold honey as well. Swansie is gone now but his legacy lives on under new ownership as Old Orchard Creek Blueberry Farm.

In Warrensville there were two apple orchards on Stanley Road during the middle of the twentieth century owned and operated by unrelated Stanleys, Virgil and Thomas.

Another popular small orchard was the Robert McNeil orchard on 221 North just south of Joe Gentry Road.

During the 1920s and '30s the Daugherty family had a substantial apple orchard on Flatwoods Road. They hauled their apples by horse and wagon as far away as Johnson City, Tennessee, and people came from miles around to buy apples at their apple barn. Clara Daugherty lived well into her nineties and had a favorite cooking apple dubbed "Clara's Creek" apple because it grew on a creek bank and it belonged to her. The medium sized yellow apple is firm, crisp and sweet and was her favorite apple to make fruit and eggs with. Clara allowed Big Horse Creek Farm to take sign wood from her tree to continue its heritage and tradition of fried apples and eggs.

Introduced and escaped trees are now as big a part of Ashe County culture and history as the native trees. They have become so intertwined they are inseparable. In the continuing quest for beauty, food and materials and with the changing climate more and more trees will be developed and introduced to Ashe County. A thousand years from now there is no telling what the trees and forests will look like but if anyone then is interested in what is going on in the early part of the twenty-first century, maybe a copy of this book will survive and let them know.

Force of Nature

The trees of Ashe County are a force of nature. Their presence is a stunning example of what it means to be bigger than life. Standing next to a great old tree is awe inspiring. Contemplating its age in hundreds of years and all that has taken place in its lifetime is mesmerizing. There are no other plants more important to our general health and well being than trees. Trees are air quality control. They reach up into the atmosphere absorbing carbon and, amazingly, pour oxygen back out. They perform this incredible exchange with beauty and anonymity.

Without trees Ashe County would look a lot like the Scottish Highlands, not bad, but extremely barren of trees. There are some advantages to having no trees. There would be no leaves to rake, no gutters to clean. Deer would be easier to spot before they jumped in front of your car. Solar panels and windmills would perform at maximum potential. There would be no stumps to grind. There would be plenty of meadows and pasture for animal husbandry. Septic tanks would not get clogged by tree roots. There would be no roadblocks holding up traffic while crews cut trees back from the highway. Fisherman wouldn't get their hooks caught in overhanging limbs. There would be no squirrels raiding your bird feeder or digging up your flower bulbs. No trees to run into if your car ran off the road. Trees wouldn't fall on your house, across your driveway or on your vehicles. Pollarding trees wouldn't be possible. Kids wouldn't be tempted to smoke Catawba tree beans. Trees would not impede the trajectory of your golf ball or Frisbee. There would be fewer power outages. Kittens would not get stuck up in a tree. No tree frogs peeping a chaotic chorus. No coons to tree. More wide open scenery. More skiable slopes. No sticks or pine cones to pick up after storm. No kites hung up in a tree. No firewood to cut and split. No trees falling in the woods that nobody hears. Even with all these resplendent advantages to having no trees, Ashe County without trees is unimaginable.

Ashe County is one of the most beautiful places in the world. Last check, it was tied for first place with all the other most beautiful places in the world. Trees energize the landscape like electricity energizes our homes, businesses, schools and farms. Their value is complex, almost beyond comprehension. From the microbiology they host and interact with, to the birds, mammals, reptiles, amphibians, insects and arachnids they share habitat with, to their transpiration of gases and vapors, to the erosion they prevent, and their nearly limitless practical, emotional and psychological value to us humans, trees hold Ashe County together. Trees don't keep time, they spend it lavishly on themselves. They are in no hurry, they are in the moment, a repository of the past and the possibility of the future.

This Black Birch Tree is not going to be denied taking root on difficult terrain.

Trees are a force of nature and a magnificent display of survival in daunting circumstances, while becoming an art form.

A child building a treehouse is one of the most memorable experiences of childhood. A treehouse is a kid's first encounter with having their very own place. Up in a treehouse, looking down on the world from a private perch, gives a child their first glimpse of their autonomy and what it means to be on their own. The tree seems to be secondary to the self-awareness unfolding in its branches but unwittingly the child is also having a first intimate relationship with a tree. Being up in the tree canopy among the branches and leaves is a much different association with a tree than standing on the ground looking up at its trunk. The look and feel of the bark going hand over hand, foothold over foothold climbing up, the smell of crushed leaves and the tingle of the fear of falling all give countenance and gravity to the relationship of child and tree. In a short while the fear is gone, the familiarity with the tree's branching is second nature and the little treehouse becomes a haven in the sky.

A kids tree house almost hidden from view by the trees around it, abandoned and falling apart, but once a place to play.

Children do not intellectually contemplate trees but, instead, interact with them innocently with the matter of factness of an enlightened being. They collect colorful leaves in the fall like art. They pick up sticks and start whacking tall weeds, mowing them down indiscriminately. They gather bigger sticks and make teepees out of them. They build shelters and forts with pine boughs or discarded Christmas trees. Children climb trees instinctively. They discover climbing trees in small low branching trees and then move on to bigger trees that have ladder-like branching like white pine. Then they learn to shinny up a limbless trunk hugging it with arms and legs and scooting upward like an inchworm. Old hollow trees make good hideouts. Trees too big to shinny up or climb? No problem, a resourceful kid will find some boards and nail them to the trunk for a ladder. Trees are pied pipers calling children to them for adventure and intrigue.

In Ashe County trees and wood are everywhere and so are the folks who

Wheeler Munroe (circa 2000), climbing around up in a huge old White Oak, giving it a hug.

make their living and hobbies from trees and wood: nurserymen, landscapers, Christmas tree growers, carpenters, furniture makers, luthiers, craftsmen, loggers, beekeepers, millers, cabinet makers, sculptors and maple syrup producers. It is hard to imagine what people do in places where there are no trees. They sure can't sit in the shade of a tree and contemplate life without trees.

Christmas Tree Farming

    Christmas tree farming is big business in Ashe County and greases the many wheels of commerce associated with it. Whether it be land acquisition (buying or leasing), banking, insurance, taxes, government agricultural extension programs, jobs, legal and illegal immigrant labor, machinery, machinery repair, trucks, trailers, irrigation, chemical fertilizers, pesticides, herbicides and fuel, there is a lot to keep up with growing Christmas trees and no matter how organized and prepared the farmer, mother nature can wreak havoc on the best laid plans.

    Consider growing Christmas trees in the abstract. As an agricultural enterprise it is a cultural phenomenon unlike any other. Sure, folks have been cutting down evergreen trees and bringing them indoors to decorate and celebrate one holiday or another for a long time. Evergreens are attractive and smell good. It is an innocent enough custom and there is fun to be found in the tradition. In days of old, trees were cut from the wild with an axe and dragged home by the trunk. Back then nobody grew Christmas trees for sale. In the 1900 census there were only 76,212,168 people living in the United States, so there were plenty of Christmas trees growing in the wild for everyone who wanted one to go cut one down. But now there are four and a half times that many people and not enough wild trees to supply the demand. Also, in 1900 more folks lived in the country than in cities. Now that has flipped and there aren't many wild evergreens growing in the city. You can't just go out and cut one down. Besides that, not everyone owns an axe these days. Thus the beginning of Christmas tree farming. There was money to be made. Not hard to understand. Almost every farmer has more than one poker in the fire. But what is intellectually difficult to get a grip on is spending ten to fifteen years growing a tree, cutting it down, killing it (they don't grow back from the stump), selling it to someone who displays it for a few weeks and

Christmas Tree farming is all about growing Fraser Fir by the tens of thousands and shipping them all over the country.

then throws it away. All those years, energy and land to grow something to throw away. Yikes. Somebody needs to come up with an edible Christmas tree.

And then there is the Christmas tree lot, another cultural phenomenon. You don't have to be a Christmas tree grower to have a Christmas tree lot, though many growers do set up their own lots. Christmas tree sales for non-profit organizations are an annual fund raising strategy as well as for entrepreneurs looking to make a fast buck.

Every year around Thanksgiving, Christmas tree lots pop up on vacant lots and parking lots all over the country, particularly in cities, selling all kinds of Christmas-related decorations. Not only do they sell Christmas trees of all sizes, they sell wreaths, garland, mistletoe, holly boughs, pine cones and red ribbons. But the most important and popular item they sell is the Fraser fir and Ashe County farmers grow more of them than anywhere else in the world. A Christmas tree lot is a fun and fragrant place to shop. Picking out a Christmas tree is usually a family affair so there are a lot of excited kids running around hollering out "Look at this one." The trees are displayed individually, set up like a miniature boreal forest so they can be walked between and around, viewed like participants in a beauty pageant. Picking out the tree is the fun, easy part of the affair. An eight foot Fraser fir is a large, heavy mass of wood and vegetation that can weigh well over a hundred pounds. Getting it off the roof or out of the hatchback, attaching a stand and getting it stood up is no small feat. In a way, going to a Christmas tree lot, picking out a tree, driving it home and cutting a slice off the butt of the tree to let it draw water better from the stand reservoir simulates going out into the wild and cutting down a tree. It is a very satisfying family event.

In Ashe County many tree farms offer choose and cut trees for customers. It has been a popular pilgrimage for many families to head to Ashe County from off the mountain to buy a tree instead of from a Christmas tree lot. This way folks can have an excursion up into the High Country where the air is clean and cold, wander around a tree farm with thousands of trees to choose from, view the beautiful mountain scenery, catch a meal in West Jefferson, stroll the shops and galleries and have great family fun.

Anyone who has ever grown Fraser fir trees will tell you, it ain't easy. Even though you see millions of them growing in Ashe County, the sweat equity is high, management is long term, the labor force is large, the equipment is expensive, the pesticides and herbicides are dangerous, the fertilizer is heavy, the slope is steep and mother nature is a quirky old lady. Nonetheless, there is money to be made in Christmas trees for the patient farmer and nobody does it better than Ashe County farmers.

As the years have gone by and more and more farmers grow Christmas trees, it has become complicated to do. Growing Fraser fir together in fields of tens of thousands at a time can be described as monoculture which makes for easier management but invites infestations of insects and fungi that are difficult to control. In the infancy of Fraser fir farming there were few problems to contend with. Fraser firs were once used as ornamental trees in the landscape and grew into big shade trees. They were a favorite climbing tree for children with their regular branching and could be climbed all the way to the top. Old Fraser firs had blisters full of gooey, sticky, sweet-smelling sap. Kids would pop the blisters and smear it on themselves because it smelled

Henry A. Garfield hauling a Christmas Tree cut from the wild in 1950, with axe in hand and gun under his arm in case he sees a deer (photographer unknown).

so good and kids do that kind of stuff. But no more. Fraser fir have so many pest problems now, mature ones are rare. They would have to be sprayed top to bottom annually to protect them from pests just like they are sprayed on Christmas tree plantations.

A number of strategies have been tried over the years to control pests, fungi and weeds. Farmers have tried grazing sheep among them to eat the grass and weeds but sheep like to lie down on the low branches and it damages the tree. Geese have been used too, but bobcats, coyotes and fox like the taste of goose. Ladybugs have been introduced *en masse* to eat aphids and adelgids but ladybugs like to winter over and lay eggs in heated houses and blooms of ladybugs indoors are a seasonal mess and annoyance. There is no cure for root rot other than planting Fraser fir on slopes where water will run off; they don't like wet feet. As more and different pests and fungi find the densely planted trees to their liking, new chemicals have to be invented to protect the crop. Some of these chemicals have had unwanted residual effects such as polluting water, killing beneficial insects and erosion. Steep ground sprayed with herbicide is asking for trouble. Runoff of fertilizers, pesticides and herbicides has a cause and effect that has to be tiptoed around very carefully. It is not cost effective to plant Fraser firs farther apart to allow mowing between trees. Mowing between rows was once a common weed control strategy but it wasn't totally effective, especially on young trees and it was expensive. There doesn't appear to be any silver bullet to solve Fraser fir management problems other than not growing them on such a large scale, densely packed, but that's not going to happen, not when there is money to be made in spite of all the problems.

Landscaping

Landscaping is a trade, a craft and an art. As its name implies it begins with the land. Drainage is first on the list when it comes to preparing a site. Rainwater and streams need to enter the site and leave the site in such a way that heavy rain or even flooding does little or no damage. This can be accomplished by opening up the drainage and spreading the water across the landscape or by funneling it via a swale or rock lined ditch. If a stream is part of the landscape it would need to be reinforced with boulders, trees and shrubs to keep it from washing out.

Landscape design is the art of landscaping. Any given site lends itself to what can be done. If the site is treeless, the first order of business is the placing of trees. And the variety of trees. The placing of trees is often dictated by the amount of space available, soil type, moisture in the soil, desire for shade, privacy, wind break, and focal points. Planting the right tree in the right place is a big deal. If you plant a tree in the wrong place and have invested twenty years in its development, then discover it was a mistake, it can be expensive to remove, expensive to replace and you've lost twenty years. Choosing the right trees needs experience and research. That's where the landscape designer comes in. There are so many trees to choose from in any given landscape that it ultimately boils down to aesthetics, and preference. That's where the research comes in. Look the tree up, ask how big will it get in twenty years? Fifty years? How wide will it spread? Evergreen or deciduous? Flowering or fruiting? Messiness? Hardiness? Color? Diseases? Poisonous? Attracts birds? Aroma? Pruning? Water tolerance? Drought tolerance? How to feed the tree and how much? Which fertilizer? Does it need to be watered? How long? When is the best time to plant? In Ashe County November is the best time to plant a tree. By then the tree is dormant as far as putting out new growth. The ground hasn't started to freeze and there is usually good

There are endless possibilities and combinations of plants and materials for building a landscape and over time it is one long roll of revelation.

ground moisture. Even though the top of the tree is dormant, the tree will begin to put out new roots and by spring the tree will have an established root system that will not require watering unless there is a drought. When planting trees the only fertilizer needed is phosphate. Phosphate stimulates root development and bud set. In the spring, late March, add a balanced fertilizer that is slow release.

If the landscape site is wooded the only grading and draining work will be done around any architectural features. On a wooded site the grade will mostly be left intact. There are several ways to deal with a wooded site. Leave it as it is in its natural state; thin the trees out to give them more room and sunlight; or bulldoze them and start over. Bulldozing is not a good alternative. The site then becomes vulnerable to erosion and a lot of topsoil will be lost. Trees are usually cut down before they are dozed, then the stumps have to be removed. Sometimes the trees can be sold to a sawmill, depending on how big they are and what they are, but most folks who clear a site don't bother. The trees are pushed into a pile and burned. The stumps don't burn well so they are hauled away. Then the landscape has to be regraded and replanted in something else. It is a common practice to bulldoze a site when the owner is looking for a view and then just plant it back in grass and shrubs. It works for the view but destroys natural habitat and the view of the site from away is an obvious scar on the mountain.

Leaving the wooded lot alone is the least intrusive and least expensive. Going in and thinning the trees or cutting a swath for a view is less destructive. Often big trees are left too close to structures and can cause problems down the road with limbs and trees falling on them. It is easier and less expensive to deal with those trees before a structure is built. Another strategy is to leave as much of the woods intact and every so often go in and cull out the trees that have gotten too thickly grown together or may be hollow or unhealthy. It is called forest management and if you have enough acreage in management the county offers a tax break. Check it out with the county agricultural extension agent.

When looking at a wooded land to be built upon or developed, it is a good idea to have professional advice. There have been many sites butchered unnecessarily and to great expense not only to the owner but to the habitat being destroyed. Everyone it seems comes to Ashe County because they are captivated by its beauty. Help protect that beauty by being aware of what makes it beautiful and meld with it instead of destroying it. A good example of what not to do is the "miracle mile" or big box construction, billboards, and parking lots along 221 between West Jefferson and Jefferson. A tree planting plan should be required but isn't. Parking lots and roadways should be tree-lined with appropriate, long lived varieties. Trees should be sacrosanct in Ashe County. When they have to be removed, they should be planted back as much as possible. Islands of trees in parking lots should be left in place or planted back so they can offer shade and cut down on runoff from parking lots. County planners should do everything in their power to protect trees and require developers to plant trees in meaningful numbers on their construction sites. There should be tree ordinances here in this land of trees. Because there are so many does not mean they can be indiscriminately destroyed and disrespected. Ashe County's most important resource is its land and trees and they should be honored and protected as such. If millions of dollars can be spent building a major highway into the county, there should be plenty of money for replacing some of the trees and it should be done in accordance with what was destroyed. Native trees should be planted randomly all along the new highway instead of introduced ornamental trees. The natural balance of trees along the highway should be restored wherever possible. Rows of trees should be avoided in deference to the mixed hardwood forest that used to line the highway. Native oaks, maples, hickory, magnolia, basswood, black gum, dogwood, serviceberry, beech, sassafras, white pine, black walnut, birch, hornbeam, wild cherry, sumac, sourwood, hawthorn and witch hazel should be planted. Respect for our native forest should be the rule, not the exception.

Ashe County is a paradisiacal place to live. More and more people are finding that to be true. It is no longer the lost province. A major highway is being gouged across the county to deliver more people, cars and trucks at a faster rate. More houses will be built. More trees cut down. The towns will grow. The powers that be have passed up opportunities to require new businesses to plant trees on their building sites. We remember Joni Mitchell and her "pave paradise and put up a parking lot." Paradise can be lost without vigilance. Stewardship of this magnificent forested land is everyone's responsibility and we must hand it down to the generations to come with tender, loving care.

INDEX

Numbers in ***bold italics*** indicate pages with photographs

Alanthus 119
Alaskan Cedar 119, 144, 150, 153, ***154***
Alleghany County 3
allelopathic 44
American Beech 28, 34, 35, ***37***, ***38***
American Chestnut 5, 17, 23, ***23***, ***25***, 26, 27, 28, 29, 32, ***35***, 36
American Holly 13, 14, ***14***
American Indians *see* Native Americans
American Plane Tree 75
American White Ash 92, 93
Appalachian Mountains 124, 195
apple trees 120, 124, 125, 227, ***228***, 229, 230
apples (heirloom) 229
Arborvitae 119, ***157***, 158
Aristocrat Pear 188
Arts Council 122
Ash Leaf Maples 119, 222
Ashe County Court House 134
Ashe County farmers 237, 238
Ashe County Farmers Market 226, 227
Ashe County Park 109
Ashe County Public Library 182, ***183***
Ashe Memorial Hospital 144
Ashe Services for Aging 128
Asian Birch 120, ***186***, ***187***
Asian Spruce 120
Atlantic Cedar 119, 147, ***147***, 156
"Aurea" 142
Autumn Flame 52

Baker Hill 119, 122
Bald Cypress 119, 133, 134, ***135***, 136
Balm of Gilead 73–74
Balsam Poplar 72, 73, 75, 78
Bam Bud 73
Bantam Chef 120, 193
Basswood 97, 244
Beard, Harry 225
Beech Trees 28, ***36***, 215, 244
beekeepers 235
Big Horse Creek Farm 227, 229, 230
Big Tooth Aspen 120, 174

Birch family ***64***, 215, 244
Black Birch ***61***, 62, ***62***, ***232***
Black Cherry 79, 81
Black Gum 98, 99, ***99***, 244
Black Maples 56, 107
Black Pine 119
Black Walnut 28, 39, 41, 42, ***42***, 43, 44, 244
Black Willow 72, ***73***, 78
Bloodgood Japanese Maple 164, 166, ***166***, 171
Blue Atlantic Cedar ***148***
Blue Beech 63, ***63***, 64, ***64***, 66
Blue Ridge Conservancy 12
Blue Ridge Elementary School 119
Blue Ridge Parkway 4, 168, 216, 217, ***218***
Blue Ridge Women in Agriculture Farm Tour 226
Blue Spruce 139, 147
Blueberry 104
Bluff Mountain Nature Preserve 12, ***18***, 216, 217
Bom-a-Gilly 73, 74, ***74***
boreal forest 13
Boulevard Cypress 119, 150, 152, ***152***
Bradford Pear 120, ***122***, 188, ***189***, 196
Broadleaf Evergreens 13
bronze birch borer 182
Brushy Fork, NC ***96***
Bryson City, NC 69
Buck Mountain Road ***5***
Buckeye 3, 28, 39, ***40***, ***41***, 206
Buffalo Road 9, 176, ***143***
Butternut 28, 39, 44
Buttonwood 75

cabinet makers 235
Camp, Lisa ***163***, ***211***, ***218***
Canada 4
Carolina Hemlock 13, 17, ***18***
Carolina Silver Bell 119
carpenters 235
Catawba 119, 120, 193, ***193***
catkins (male flowers) 45, ***45***
"cedar" 145
Cherry 124, ***124***, 125, ***206***

245

Index

The author undergoes a tree-cuddling (circa 2001).

chestnut blight 25, 27
Chestnut Oak 24, 28, 32, *35*
Chinese Ailanthus 173
Chinese Chestnut 26, 120, 189, *190*, 191, *191*, 192
Chinese Fir 119
Chinquapin 28, 29, 35
Choke Cherries 79, 80, *81*
Christmas Tree farming 120, 215, 235, 236, 237, *237*, 239
Christmas Trees 2, 18, 127, *162*, 200, 203, 209, 214, 217, 238, *239*
Clampitt, Kelly *33*, *37*, *55*, *58*, *68*, *73*, *76*, *86*, *94*, *104*, *105*, *121*, *140*, *162*, *193*, *209*
"Clara's Creek" apple 230
Clifton, NC *146*, *199*, 226, 229, *55*, *74*
Coastal Plain 171
Colorado Blue Spruce 119, 137, 141
Columbus, Christopher 134
Colvard Oil Company 120
Concolor Fir 120, *160*
conifers 13, 209
Copeland Road 229
coppices *86*
Cottonwood 120, 177, *178*, 179, *179*
craftsmen 235
Crepe myrtles 171
Creston, NC *61*, *76*, *87*, 122, 215, *216*
Crimson King Norway Maple 119, 180, *181*
Cripps Cypress 119, 150, *152*, 153
Cucumber Tree 67, 69, 70, 71, *71*

Daugherty, Clara 230
Daugherty family 230
Dawn Redwood 119, 131, *131*, *132*, 133, 134
Deodara Cedar 120, 146, *146*, 147
Dog Hobble 104
Dogwood Tree *see* Flowering Dogwood
Dwarf Willow 59

eagles 9
Eastern Continental Divide of North America 4, *218*
Eastern Hemlock *5*, *6*, 7, 13, 17
Ed Little Road *74*
Elderberry 223, *223*, *224*
elk 9
Elk Knob 137
Elliot Road 176
emerald ash borer 93
"emerald green giant" 158
English garden 150
European Birch 120, 182, *184*, *185*
European Cherry 119, 126
European settlers 9, 27, 219, 227

"False Cypress" 150
Fernspray Cypress 119
Flatwoods Road 230
Florence Thomas Art School 51
Flowering Cherry 119, 164, *165*, 171
Flowering Crabapple 120
Flowering Dogwood 7, 113, *114*, 115, *115*, 116, *170*, 244
"Forest Pansy" 169
Franklin, Robbie *61*, *62*, *186*, *187*
Fraser Fir 7, 19, 120, *162*, *163*, 199, 200, *201*, 214, 237, *237*, 238, 239, 240
Fringe Tree 119, 164, 167, *167*, 168, *168*, 171
Full Moon Maple 120
furniture makers 235

Garfield, Henry A. *239*
Gauguin, Paul 17
Georgia 25
Ginkgo tree 120, 127, 128, *128*, *129*, 130, 131
global warming 120
Golden Chain Tree 120
Golden Raintree 120
Goosefoot 3
"Gowdy" 142
Green Leaf Redbud 168

Hadley, Kim *5*, *6*, *11*, *18*, *25*, *30*, *31*, *60*, *110*, *175*, *183*, *208*, *216*, *225*
Hassinger Lumber Company 24

Hawthorn 101, *101*, 102, *102*, 103, 244
Heath family 104
hells *16*
hemlock woolly adelgid *6*, 17
Hickory 45, 244
Highway 221 120
Highway 88 *33*, 119, 123, *146*, 176, 229
Hinoki Cypress 120, 150, *151*, *152*
Hophornbeam 3, 63, *65*, 66, *66*, 244
"Husk spice" 229
"Husk Sweet" 229
Hybrid Poplar 119

Industrial Revolution 10
Ironwood 3, 63, 64, *64*

Japanese Maple 119, 164, *166*
Jefferson, NC *33*, 120, 122, *124*
Jefferson Avenue 120, 121, 134, 193, *193*
Joe Gentry Road 230
Johnson City, TN 230
Jonasee Rock *199*
Joyce Kilmer Memorial Forest 69
Joyner, Ron *19*, 229
Joyner, Suzanne (Sue) *19*, 229
Juniper *144*

Kousa Dogwood 120, 164, 169, 170, 171
Kudzu 119

landscapers 235
Lansing, NC 120, *145*
legume family 107
Lemon Thread Cypress 119
Leviton Manufacturing Company 121
Leyland Cypress 119, 153, *155*
Lihue Knob *225*
Linden trees *95*, 96, *96*, 97
Locust *107*, *108*
loggers 235
Lombardy Poplar 120
luthiers 235

magnolia 244
Mahler, Lissy *129*
maiden hair tree 128
Maine 25
maple keys *52*
maple syrup 44, 49, 197, 219, 220, 222, 225, 226, 235
maple trees 43, 90, 126, *213*, 215, *220*, 221, 222, 244, 226
McConnell Street *195*
McGee, Marty *54*, *77*, *96*, *141*
Miller, Rex *114*
millers 235
Mimosa 119, 173, *174*

Molley Chomper Cidery 229
Momi Fir *161*
Monterey Cypress 153
Mother nature 126
Mount Jefferson 213
Mount Jefferson State Park [now Mount Jefferson State Natural Area] 174, 216, 217
Mount Rogers 4, 137
Mountain Ash 59, 92, 93, *94*, 215
Mountain Holly 13
Mountain Laurel 104
mountain lions 9
Mountain Maple 56, 59
Mud Maple 75
Multiflora Rose 103, 119
Munroe, Doug *21*, *50*, *61*, *199*, *200*, *201*, *203*, *213*, *220*, *237*, *242*
Munroe, Wheeler *132*, *221*, *235*

Native Americans 9, 10, 27, 88, 125, 219
Nature Conservancy 12, *18*, 216, 217
Nellie Stevens Holly 120
New River 9
New River (north fork) 4, *74*, *76*, *177*, 229
New River (south fork) 4, *208*, *211*
New River Conservancy 12
New River State Parks 216
North America 127
North Carolina 3, 12
North Carolina Department of Agriculture 226
Northern Red Oak 28, 32, *33*, *34*
Norway maples 222
Norway Spruce 119, 139, 141
nurseries and nurserymen 204, 235

Oaks *11*, 126, 215, 244
October Glory 52
Old 16 123
Old Field Creek Road 75
old growth forest 125
Old Methuselah 134
Old Norway Spruce *140*, *141*
Old Orchard Creek Blueberry Farm 230
Oriental Spruce 142, *143*
Ornamental tree nurseries 202
Osborne, Linda *87*
otters 9

Paddy Mountain 213, 216, 217
Paper Birch 185
Paperbark Maple 120
Paulownia 120, *175*, 176
Peach 120
The Peak (Creston) *61*, 216, 217
Pear 120
Phoenix Mountain 216

Index

Piedmont 153, 171
Pignut Hickory 28, 39, 45, *45*, *46*
Pin Cherry 79, 80
pines 13, 18
Pollarding trees 121, *121*, *122*
Pond Mountain game land 215, 216
Pope, Scot *235*
Purple Beech 120
Purple Leaf Plum 119, 164, 171

Radio Hill 169
Raulston, Dr. J.C. 188
Ray Taylor Road 128
Red Cedar 144, *144*, *145*
Red Maple 49, *49*, *50*, 51, *52*, 56, *83*, 207, 220, 222
Red Maple flowers (Female) *49*, (Male) *51*
Red Spruce 137
Red Sunset 52
Redbud 120, 164, 168, *169*, 171
"Redwood of the East" 26
Rembert, Betty *1*, *2*, *3*, *10*, *14*, *15*, *16*, *20*, *23*, *24*, *34*, *35*, *36*, *38*, *40*, *41*, *42*, *45*, *46*, *47*, *57*, *63*, *64*, *65*, *66*, *69*, *70*, *71*, *74*, *80*, *81*, *85*, *89*, *90*, *92*, *95*, *98*, *99*, *101*, *102*, *107*, *108*, *111*, *113*, *115*, *122*, *128*, *131*, *132*, *135*, *138*, *144*, *145*, *146*, *147*, *148*, *151*, *152*, *154*, *155*, *157*, *160*, *165*, *167*, *168*, *169*, *170*, *172*, *174*, *177*, *178*, *179*, *181*, *184*, *185*, *189*, *190*, *191*, *195*, *196*, *202*, *206*, *207*, *210*, *221*, *223*, *224*, *228*, *232*, *233*, *234*
Rembert, George, II *49*, *51*, *52*, *53*, *58*, *83*
Rhododendron 104, 215
River Birch 120, 182, *183*
River House Inn 75, *77*
Robert McNeil orchard 230
Roberts, Adam *19*
Roberts, Cheryl *129*
Robinson, Joe 122, *140*, *141*
Rose of Sharon 164, 171, *172*
Rosebay Rhododendron 13, 15, *15*, *16*, 104
Roten, Nancy *84*, *87*, *143*, *161*

sarsaparilla 88
Sarvis 3
Saskatoon 3, 88
Sassafras 3, 85, *85*, *86*, 87, *87*, 88, 244
Savely, Jimmy *96*
Sawtooth Oak 120
Scotch Irish 124, 125
Scotch Pine 120
sculptors 235
2nd Street, West Jefferson 120
Serviceberry 82, 83, *83*, 84, *84*, 207, 244
Shadblow 3
Shagbark Hickory 28, 39, 45, *47*

Silver Maple 120, 195, ***195***, ***196***, 197, 222
Skyline Telephone Company 169
Slippery Elm 120
Smoke Tree 120
Soft Maple 52
Sourwood seeds *104*
Sourwood tree 96, 104, 105, *105*, 109, 244
southern Appalachian mountains *24*, 137
Staghorn Sumac 89, *89*, 90, *90*, 91, 222, 223
Striped Maple 56, *57*, 58, *58*
Sturgill 229
Styrax 119
Sugar House *220*
Sugar Maple 41, *50*, 52, 53, *53*, 54, *54*, 55, *55*, 56, 100, 120, 126, *141*, *207*, 219, 220, 221
Sumac 244
Swamp Maple 52
Sweet Birch 62
Sycamore 72, 75, *76*, 77, *77*, 78

Table Mountain Pine 13, 21, *21*, 22
Taps *223*
Tennessee 3, 4, 158
Tennessee, Virginia line 215
Thomasville Furniture Plant 229
Thompson Blue Spruce *138*, 139
Three Top Mountain/game land 215, 216, *216*
tree farms 238
treehouse 233
Tulip Tree flowers 67, 68, *68*, 69
Tupelo honey 100
Tupelo 3, 96, 98, *98*, 100
221 North 230

Virginia 3, 4
Virginia-Carolina railway 10
Virginia Creeper (train) 24
Virginia Pine 13, 21

Wahoo 3, 67, 69, *69*, 70, *70*
Warrensville, NC 119, 215, *216*, 226
Watauga County 3, 4, 137
Waterfall Farm *220*, 226
Weeping Cherry 119
Weeping Willow 72, 119, 177, *177*, 179, 206
West Jefferson, NC 51, 120, 122, 123, 134, *193*, 194, 213, 217, 229, 238
West Jefferson Park *183*
White Ash *92*
White Oak 28, 29, 32, 41, 100, *235*
White Pine 13, 18, 19, *19*, *20*, 21, 200, 201, 234, 244
White Spruce 120, 141, 142

White Walnut 44
Whitetop Mountain 4, 137
Wild Cherry 41, *50*, 79, *80*, 244
Wilkes County 3
Winecoff, Tim and Judith *135*
Witch Hazel 110, *110*, 111, *111*, 112, 244
Wollemia Pine 131, 133

wolves 9
Worth, David 123

Yellow Birch 60, *60*
Yellow Locust 7, 107, 108, 109
Yellow Wood 119